• T R O P H I E S •

Language Handbook

Grade 4

Printed in the United States of America

ISBN 0-15-325066-6

9 10 073 10 09 08 07 06 05 04

Harcourt

Orlando   Boston   Dallas   Chicago   San Diego

Visit *The Learning Site!*
www.harcourtschool.com

CONTENTS

Visit *The Learning Site!*
www.harcourtschool.com

contents

Contents

Your Best Writing

Many people think writing is difficult. They do not realize that it is easy to become a better writer! This handbook will give you the skills, strategies, tips, and models you need to become the best writer you can be. Let's start with an overview of writing and writing strategies.

The Writing Process

When you look at a book, you do not see the process the writer used to make it. What you see in print might not be much like the first plan for the book. The author might have rewritten the book several times.

The writing process is often divided into five stages. Most writers go back and forth through these stages. There is no one correct way to write.

Writing for Tests

When you write for a test, you usually don't follow all the steps of the writing process. Here are a few tips that can help you with test taking:

- Study the prompt carefully.
- Plan ahead.
- Keep track of the time.

For more about test taking, see pages 52–54. ➡

Prewriting

In this stage, you plan what you are going to write. You choose a topic, identify your audience, brainstorm ideas, and organize information.

Drafting

In this stage, you write your ideas in sentences and paragraphs. Follow your prewriting plan to write a first draft of your composition.

Revising

This stage is the first part of editing your writing. You may work by yourself or with a partner or a group. Make changes that will improve your writing.

Proofreading

In this stage, you finish your editing by polishing your work. Check for errors in grammar, spelling, capitalization, and punctuation. Make a final copy of your composition.

Publishing

Finally, you choose a way to present your work to an audience. You may want to add pictures, make a class book, or read your work aloud.

Keeping a Writer's Journal

Many writers keep journals. In your journal, you can list your ideas for writing. You can also write freely, draw pictures, keep notes, and experiment with words.

To start your own writer's journal, choose a notebook. Decorate the cover if you wish. Then start filling the pages with your notes and ideas.

You may want to keep a **Word Bank** at the back of your journal. Here you can list different kinds of words to use in your writing, such as science words, sports words, colorful adjectives, and strong verbs.

Reading ↔ Writing Connection

You read many different kinds of material each day. Pay attention to text on the television, in advertisements, on the Internet, and, of course, in books and articles. When you see an interesting word or phrase, jot it down in your Word Bank.

Keeping a Portfolio

A portfolio is a collection of work, such as samples of writing, drawings, and photographs. It is sometimes used to show a person's work to others.

Student writers often keep two types of portfolios. **Working portfolios** include writing on which you are still working. **Show portfolios** have pieces of writing that you are ready to show to others.

You can use either kind of portfolio when you have writing conferences with other students or your teacher. In a writing conference, talk about your work. Tell what you are doing and what you like doing. Set goals for yourself as a writer.

Writer's Craft

Writing well means more than just "following the rules," or writing what a teacher or a test tells you to write. Think about any game or sport you like to play. Yes, following the rules is important. However, to play well, you need to use special skills and strategies. In basketball, for example, a player needs to pass well, run quickly, and defend the basket.

Good writing takes special skills and strategies, too. This web shows the traits, or characteristics, of good writing. You will learn much more about these traits in this handbook.

The Traits of Good Writing

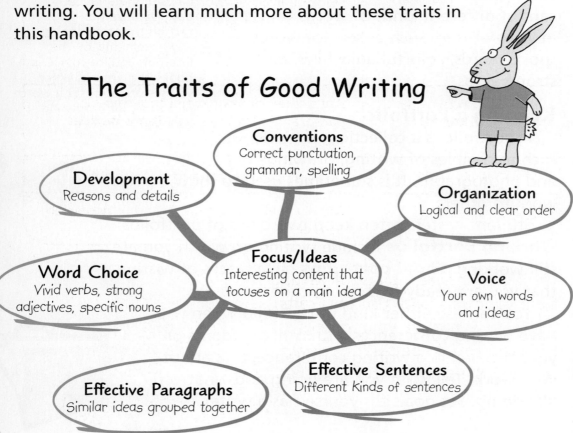

Conventions
Correct punctuation, grammar, spelling

Development
Reasons and details

Organization
Logical and clear order

Word Choice
Vivid verbs, strong adjectives, specific nouns

Focus/Ideas
Interesting content that focuses on a main idea

Voice
Your own words and ideas

Effective Paragraphs
Similar ideas grouped together

Effective Sentences
Different kinds of sentences

Traits Checklist

Good writers practice, practice, practice! As you practice, ask yourself these questions.

☑ **FOCUS/IDEAS**	Is my purpose clear? Do I stay on the topic?
☑ **ORGANIZATION**	Are my ideas in a clear order? Does my writing have a beginning, a middle, and an ending?
☑ **DEVELOPMENT**	Do I use details and reasons to support my ideas?
☑ **VOICE**	Do I use my own words? Do I seem to care about my topic and my audience?
☑ **EFFECTIVE SENTENCES**	Do I use a variety of sentence types?
☑ **EFFECTIVE PARAGRAPHS**	Are similar ideas grouped together in paragraphs? Do I use transitions, such as time-order words?
☑ **WORD CHOICE**	Do I use exact nouns and strong verbs?
☑ **CONVENTIONS**	Are my spelling, grammar, and punctuation correct?

Try This! Choose a piece of writing from your portfolio. Use the Traits Checklist. What are your strengths? How can you do better? Jot down your ideas in your Writer's Journal.

Focus/Ideas

Before you begin to write, you must decide on your purpose and your main idea. Do you want to entertain your readers with a story, inform them about an interesting topic, or persuade them to do something? What is the main thing you want to say? When you make these decisions, you are choosing the **focus** of your writing. You should keep your focus in mind as you write.

Read this student's paragraph that compares. Think about how the writer stays focused on the topic.

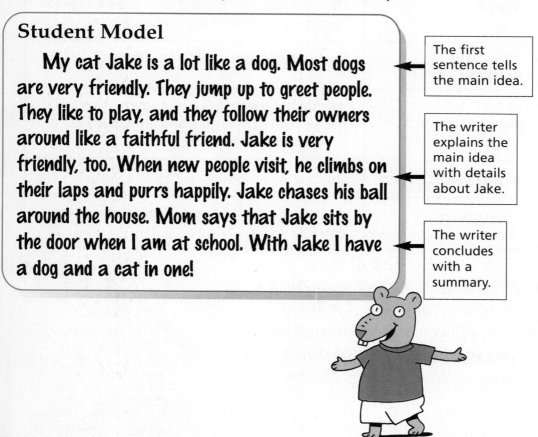

Student Model

My cat Jake is a lot like a dog. Most dogs are very friendly. They jump up to greet people. They like to play, and they follow their owners around like a faithful friend. Jake is very friendly, too. When new people visit, he climbs on their laps and purrs happily. Jake chases his ball around the house. Mom says that Jake sits by the door when I am at school. With Jake I have a dog and a cat in one!

The first sentence tells the main idea.

The writer explains the main idea with details about Jake.

The writer concludes with a summary.

How to Focus Your Writing

Strategies	How to Use the Strategies	Examples
• **Narrow your topic.**	• Make sure your topic is not too broad.	• Narrow the topic "cats" to "my cat, Jake."
• **Keep your purpose in mind.**	• Stick to your purpose of entertaining, informing or persuading.	• Give readers entertaining details about a pet's actions.
• **Stay on the topic.**	• Make sure each detail relates directly to the topic.	• Explain the main idea, "My cat Jake is a lot like a dog," with details that show the similarities.

Try This! Choose one of these topics: camping, dinosaurs, or fireworks. List several ways you might get ideas about the topic. Tell what the purpose of a piece of writing on this topic might be.

Reading ↔ Writing Connection

Find a magazine article on a topic that interests you. State the purpose and the main idea of the article. Tell whether the writer stays focused on the topic and how the writer might have gotten ideas for the article.

Focus/Ideas

Now it's your turn! Write an informational report that is interesting and focused.

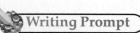

Writing Prompt

Everyone thinks about the job he or she might do as an adult. Think about jobs that interest you. Then write an informational report that tells about the job that interests you and the people who do it.

Strategies Good Writers Use

- Remember your audience and purpose.
- Explain each subtopic with interesting facts and details.

Prewrite

Make a web to plan your report.

Main Topic

Subtopic   Subtopic   Subtopic

Draft

Follow these steps to help you organize your report.

STEP 1 **Introduce the topic.** Use your first paragraph to introduce your main topic.

STEP 2 **Organize the subtopics.** Determine the order of your subtopics.

STEP 3 **Add supporting facts and details.** Start a new paragraph for each subtopic.

STEP 4 **Conclude with a summary.** Summarize your main idea in your last paragraph.

Revise

Read over the draft of your report. Use this checklist to help you revise:

☑ Have you begun each paragraph with a topic sentence?

☑ Do all the details in each paragraph tell about the topic sentence?

☑ Are there details you should leave out because they wander from the topic?

☑ Do you need to add details to make your ideas clear?

Proofread

Use this checklist as you proofread your report:

☑ Have you used capitalization and punctuation correctly?

☑ Have you indented the first line of each paragraph?

☑ Did you use a dictionary to check your spelling?

 delete text

 insert text

↰ move text

¶ new paragraph

☰ capitalize

/ lowercase

◯ correct spelling

Publish and Reflect

Make a final copy of your report, and share it with a partner. Tell what you like best about your partner's work. Discuss how you got your ideas and whether you stayed on the topic. Take notes in your Writer's Journal.

Organization

When you write, you want the information to make sense to your reader. To do this, you need to **organize** your information, or put it in a clear order. Sometimes you will need to organize your information in time order. Other times you may organize it by order of importance, putting the most important idea first or last.

Read this student's how-to essay, and think about how the writer organizes information.

Student Model

It's easy to make a miniature tornado. The materials you will need are a glass jar with a lid, water, food coloring, and some dishwashing detergent.

First, fill the jar about 3/4 of the way with water. Add a teaspoon of dishwashing detergent and as much food coloring as you need to get the color you want. Next, put the lid tightly on the jar. Shake the jar hard for about twenty seconds.

After shaking the jar, give it a quick twist. Then watch as a tiny tornado forms in the water inside the jar.

How does the writer organize this information?

What sequence words does the writer use?

How to Organize Information

Strategies	Applying the Strategies
• **Order ideas clearly.**	• Put ideas in an order that makes sense, such as time order or order of importance.
• **Use sequence words.**	• Use words such as *first, next, now,* and *after* to help readers understand sequence, or time order.

Try This! Plan a friendly letter about three things that have happened to you lately. List them in either time order or order of importance. If you use order of importance, decide whether you want to put the most important thing first or last. Explain the organization you chose.

Writing Forms

A how-to essay lists the materials needed for an activity and uses sequence words to put steps in an order that is easy to follow.

For more about how-to writing, see pages 68–69.

Organization

Now it's your turn! Write a how-to essay that puts ideas in order and is easy to follow.

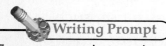
Writing Prompt

Everyone needs to take care of something. Write an essay that tells your classmates how to take care of something, such as a pet or a garden.

Prewrite

Choose one of these ways to organize your steps or main points.

sequence of steps
example:
first
next
last

Draft

Follow these steps:

STEP 1 **Introduce the task.** Try to get your audience's attention by asking a question or making a surprising statement.

STEP 2 **List any materials that are needed.** Write a sentence or two listing the materials.

STEP 3 **Explain each step or point in order.** Use sequence words that clearly show the order of the steps.

STEP 4 **Conclude with the result.** Tell about the benefits of the task.

order of importance
example:
important
more important
most important

Revise

Can you improve your essay to make it easier to understand? Use this checklist to help you revise:

☑ Will your classmates be able to follow the steps or points?

☑ Are there details you should add or leave out to make the directions easier to follow?

☑ Did you use sequence words to help your reader?

Proofread

Use this checklist as you proofread your essay:

☑ Have you used capitalization and punctuation correctly?

☑ Is each sentence complete?

☑ Did you check your spelling?

𝒑 delete text

∧ insert text

↻ move text

¶ new paragraph

≡ capitalize

/ lowercase

◯ correct spelling

Publish and Reflect

Make a final copy of your how-to essay, and share it with a partner. Read your partner's essay, and discuss what you like about it. Compare the way you and your partner organized information. Make a note in your Writer's Journal about ideas for future how-to essays.

Voice

You have your own style of doing things. You enjoy some activities and don't enjoy others. You use some words and expressions more than others. Your own way of expressing yourself in writing is called your **voice**. Your personal voice makes your writing interesting and unique. It shows that you care about your topic.

Read this student's descriptive paragraph. How does the writer show that he or she cares about the topic?

Student Model

My grandfather's boat isn't big and fancy. It is very small, just the right size for Grandpa and me. It is painted the blue of the sky on a sunny summer day. Grandpa says the motor is a cranky old mule when he tries to get it started. Once he gets it running, though, it purrs like a contented cat. I sit on the middle seat and watch the ripples the boat makes as it moves across the lake. I listen for the quick splash of the fish leaping like an acrobat. Grandpa's little blue boat is the perfect place to spend a happy afternoon.

Notice that the writer compares the color of the boat to the color of the sky.

What comparison does the writer use here?

The writer expresses his or her feelings and opinions.

Try This! Imagine you were going to draw a picture of the scene in the model. Would the picture look bright or gloomy? Would the people be happy or sad? What details would you show?

How to Develop Your Personal Voice

You can develop your personal voice by using **figurative language** and **imagery** and expressing your **viewpoint**.

Figurative language compares two different things. Some comparisons are **similes**, which use *like* or *as*. Others are **metaphors**, which say one thing is another.

Simile: Sam's bike was like a runaway horse charging down the road.   (compares bike to horse)

Metaphor: Sam's bike was a runaway horse charging down the road.   (compares bike to horse)

Imagery is using vivid language to help readers see, hear, taste, feel, or smell something. Example: Fat drops of juice shone on the cold slice of melon.

Express your own **viewpoint** to let your reader know how you feel about that subject. For example, depending on your viewpoint, you might describe a spider as *sinister* or as *magnificent*.

Try This! Find two kinds of newspaper writing: an article about world news, and an editorial. Which one shows a stronger personal voice? Support your answer with examples.

Writing Forms

A descriptive paragraph uses vivid words and figurative language to help the reader form a picture in his or her mind.

For more about descriptive writing, see pages 59–61.

➡️

Voice

Now it's your turn! Write a narrative using personal voice.

Writing Prompt

Everyone has experienced special events. Think of an event in your childhood that made you think about something in a different way. Write a personal narrative about that experience to share with your classmates.

Prewrite

Make a web like this one:

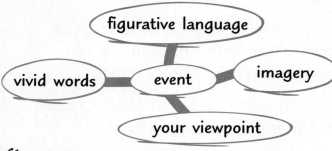

figurative language

vivid words   event   imagery

your viewpoint

Draft

Follow these steps to organize your narrative:

STEP 1 **Identify the place and time.** Establish the setting: where you were, who was there, and what you were doing.

STEP 2 **Write in your own voice.** Use comparisons and vivid language.

STEP 3 **Tell why the experience was important.** Do not just list the things you did.

Revise

Read over the draft of your personal narrative. Can you change or add anything to create a more vivid picture in your reader's mind? Use this checklist to help you revise your narrative:

☑ Do you think your readers will recognize your personal voice?

☑ Can you add figurative language or imagery?

☑ Have you expressed your viewpoint clearly?

Proofread

Use this checklist as you proofread:

☑ Have you begun sentences with capital letters?

☑ Have you used the correct end punctuation for each sentence?

☑ Did you use a dictionary to check spelling?

ℓ	delete text
∧	insert text
↫	move text
¶	new paragraph
≡	capitalize
/	lowercase
◯	correct spelling

Publish and Reflect

Make a final copy of your personal narrative, and share it with classmates in a small group. Tell what you like best about your classmates' narratives. Share ideas about how you can improve your personal narratives by using figurative language and imagery and by expressing your viewpoint. Take notes in your Writer's Journal.

Word Choice

Good writing uses **vivid words**. These are words that create clear images in the reader's mind. Strong verbs, specific nouns, and colorful adjectives make writing interesting.

Read this student's description of a person. Think about words and phrases that help you picture and understand the writer's grandmother.

Student Model

My grandmother loves cats, especially her cranky old cat named Homer. He yowls and hisses at every little thing, but my grandmother doesn't mind. She feeds him fishy-smelling cat food and brushes him every day until his fur feels smooth and silky.

Taking care of everything, including cranky cats, is what my grandmother does best. With a calm smile, she firmly shakes out her puffy quilts and listens to your troubles. Sometimes she gives advice in her soft voice hardly louder than a whisper. Mostly, though, she just listens lovingly and gives you a chance to figure out your own solutions.

Notice the use of vivid words to describe the cat.

How does the description of the cat help you better understand the writer's grandmother?

What details help you see and hear the person?

Try This! Write several sentences describing something in your classroom. Use vivid words.

Strategies for Choosing Words

Strategies	How to Use the Strategies	Examples
• **Use exact words.**	• Keep in mind that no two words have exactly the same meaning or use.	• Many interesting <u>creatures</u> live in the pond. The zoo has more than 100 kinds of <u>animals</u>.
• **Use vivid words.**	• Use strong verbs, specific nouns, and interesting adjectives and adverbs. Include details that appeal to the senses.	• verbs: *screech, leap* adjectives: *wriggly, snarly* • sensory details: *bright eyes gravelly voice soft hands scent of lilac perfume*

Reading ↔ Writing Connection

Find two stories that contain descriptions of characters. Choose several vivid words from the descriptions to add to your Word Bank.

Word Choice

Now it's your turn! Write a character sketch with vivid words.

Writing Prompt

Invent a character, and write a character sketch that could be part of a story. You might want to find a picture of an interesting-looking person in a magazine or a book of paintings and use that person as your character.

Strategies Good Writers Use

- Before writing, state your purpose in one sentence.
- Use your Word Bank to find vivid words.

Prewrite

Brainstorm details for your character sketch, and organize them in a web like this:

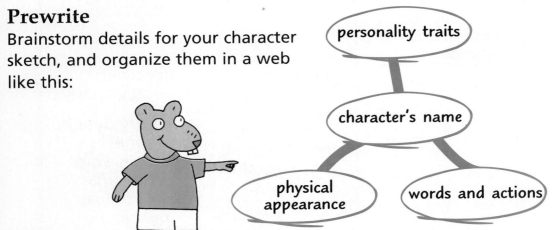

personality traits

character's name

physical appearance

words and actions

Draft

Follow these steps:

STEP 1 **Introduce your character.** Give the character's name, location, and what he or she is doing.

STEP 2 **Describe the character's appearance.**

STEP 3 **Show the character's traits**. Use the character's words and actions to show what he or she is like.

Revise

Read over the draft of your character sketch. Do you want to add, leave out, or change anything? Use this checklist to help you revise:

☑ Will your reader have a clear picture of the character?

☑ Are there any details you might add to make your character more true-to-life?

☑ Can you replace some words with more vivid ones?

ℓ	delete text
∧	insert text
↰	move text
¶	new paragraph
≡	capitalize
/	lowercase
◯	correct spelling

Proofread

Use this checklist as you proofread:

☑ Have you used capitalization and punctuation correctly?

☑ Have you used complete sentences?

☑ Did you check your spelling?

Publish and Reflect

Make a final copy of your character sketch, and share it with a partner. Compare how each of you used interesting words to help show your character's traits. Write your ideas in your Writer's Journal.

Development

The power of a piece of writing comes from the way ideas are developed. **Development** is the use of reasons and details to explain or describe. A list of the main ideas in an essay or a report would not be very interesting. It is the way a writer explains or describes the main ideas that makes the writing interesting.

Kinds of details that writers often use are descriptive details, facts, examples, and dialogue. Details may tell *who, what, when, where, why,* or *how*. Read the student model below, and see what kinds of details the writer used.

Student Model

Guinea pigs and gerbils are both rodents, but they are very different in many ways. A guinea pig is a stout animal with little, round ears and no tail. A gerbil is generally smaller and has a long tail. Guinea pigs vary in color. They may be solid white, black, or tan, or they may have light colors with streaks or blotches of darker colors. Gerbils, on the other hand, always have light tan fur. Guinea pigs originally came from South America, while gerbils are native to western Asia and Africa.

Notice the descriptive details the writer uses.

What contrast does the writer make here?

What fact does the writer conclude with?

Strategies for Development

Strategies	How to Use the Strategies	Examples
• **Use descriptive details.**	• Use details that help readers see, hear, feel, smell, or taste your subject.	• A guinea pig is a **stout** animal with **little, round** ears and **no** tail.
• **Support your ideas with facts and reasons.**	• Include answers to the questions *who, what, when, where, why,* and *how.*	• Guinea pigs come from South America, while gerbils are native to western Asia and Africa.

Try This! Choose a piece of writing from your portfolio. Look for places where you can add more details to develop your ideas. Add at least two details.

Reading ↔ Writing Connection

Find a magazine article on a topic that interests you. Point out some of the details that the writer uses to develop the topic. Choose one or two interesting facts to add to your Writer's Journal.

Development

Now it's your turn! Write an essay that uses specific details.

Writing Prompt

Write an essay for your family about the advantages and disadvantages of getting a certain kind of pet. Tell what would be good about having the pet and what some of the problems might be, and give your opinion.

> **Strategies Good Writers Use**
>
> - Identify the audience for the essay.
> - Keep in mind your purpose for writing.
> - Write a main idea that goes along with the purpose.

Prewrite

Use a chart like this one to organize your information. Include at least two advantages and two disadvantages.

Pet:	Audience:
Advantages: 1. 2.	Disadvantages: 1. 2.
Conclusion:	

Draft

Follow these steps:

STEP 1 **Introduce your topic and main idea.** Begin your essay with a catchy sentence.

STEP 2 **Organize your ideas.** Write one paragraph about the advantages and one about the disadvantages. Include details. Save the strongest part for last.

STEP 3 **Have a strong conclusion.** Restate your main idea, using different words.

Revise

Use this checklist to help you revise:

☑ Will your reader understand the advantages and disadvantages of getting the pet?

☑ Can you add reasons or details to explain or support the advantages or disadvantages?

☑ Are there details you should omit because they do not help show advantages or disadvantages?

Proofread

Use this checklist as you proofread:

☑ Have you used apostrophes correctly in contractions?

☑ Have you used the words *their, they're*, and *there; your, you're*; and *its, it's* correctly?

☑ Did you check your spelling?

ℒ	delete text
∧	insert text
↻	move text
¶	new paragraph
≡	capitalize
/	lowercase
◯	correct spelling

Publish and Reflect

Make a final copy of your essay, and share it with a partner. Discuss how to use development to improve your writing. Write your ideas in your Writer's Journal.

Effective Sentences

Effective sentences make writing easy to read. To help sentences flow smoothly, writers vary their sentences. Combining short sentences with connecting words such as *and*, *but*, and *because* also helps show how ideas are related.

Read this student's persuasive letter. Are the sentences clear, varied, and easy to read?

Student Model

Willow Road School
Springville, TX 75082
November 5, 2003

Dear Mayor Ortiz:

You are invited to a very special event. The students at Willow Road School are having a talent show in our school auditorium at 8:00 p.m. on January 10.

I know that you care about our school, and you can show your support by joining us. You can have a good time, too!

I know that you are very busy, but I hope you will mark this special date on your calendar. We would love to see you there.

Sincerely,

Jared Barnes

The writer mentions "a very special event" to capture the reader's interest.

The writer uses long and short sentences.

The writer uses the word *but* to combine sentences.

How to Write Effective Sentences

Strategies	How to Use the Strategies	Examples
• **Write a strong opening sentence.**	• Ask a question, or make a surprising statement.	• If you could change one thing about our school, what would it be?
• **Vary types of sentences.**	• Include a question, a command, or an exclamation where it fits.	• Do you want to feel better and be stronger? If so, start exercising today!
• **Vary lengths of sentences.**	• Combine short sentences for greater interest and variety.	• *Combine these sentences:* The earthquake lasted only two minutes. Those minutes seemed like hours.

Try This! Find two examples of persuasive writing in newspaper editorials, letters to the editor, or movie reviews. Find a sentence in each that you think is especially strong or effective.

Effective Sentences

Now it's your turn! Write a persuasive paragraph using effective sentences.

Writing Prompt

Everyone enjoys some kinds of hobbies or activities. Think about an activity. Then write a paragraph to persuade your classmates to try the hobby or activity.

> ***Strategies Good Writers Use***
>
> - Brainstorm a list of possible topics.
> - Explain reasons with specific details.
> - Save the strongest reason for last.

Prewrite

Use a web like this:

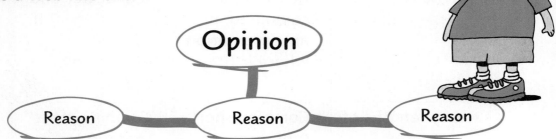

Draft

Follow these steps to write a first draft:

STEP 1 **Capture your readers' interest.** Start with an effective opening sentence. Then state your opinion.

STEP 2 **Give reasons.** Give each reason, followed by details that support it.

STEP 3 **Conclude with a call to action.** Suggest something for your readers to do.

Revise

Use this checklist to help you revise:

- ☑ Is your opening sentence strong?

- ☑ Have you used a variety of sentences?

- ☑ Is there a place where you can combine short sentences?

- ☑ Will your paragraph persuade your reader to agree with you?

Proofread

Use this checklist as you proofread:

- ☑ Have you used capitalization and punctuation correctly?

- ☑ Have you made sure that subjects and verbs agree?

- ☑ Did you use a dictionary to check your spelling?

 delete text

 insert text

move text

new paragraph

capitalize

lowercase

correct spelling

Publish and Reflect

Now make a final copy of your persuasive paragraph. Share your work by trading paragraphs with a partner. Tell whether your partner's paragraph makes you want to try the hobby or activity. Discuss whether the sentences made the writing easy to read. Write your ideas in your Writer's Journal.

Effective Paragraphs

In an **effective paragraph**, all the ideas are closely related. Many paragraphs begin with a **topic sentence** that states the main idea. The other sentences give details. Connecting words, or **transitions**, such as *first, next, also*, and *for example* help the ideas flow smoothly.

Read this student's brief research report. Think about how the writer used paragraphs.

Student Model

The Panama Canal connects the Atlantic and Pacific oceans. It is located in the country of Panama in Central America and is about 40 miles long. Before the canal was built, ships had to sail around South America to get from one ocean to the other.

It took a long time to get the Panama Canal built. Explorers in Central America had suggested the idea back in the 1500s. For hundreds of years, though, it was just a dream. Finally, in 1906, the United States Congress approved a plan. The canal was completed in the summer of 1914.

The first paragraph can answer questions such as *what, where, when, who, why*, and *how*.

A new topic needs a new paragraph.

The writer shows this sequence of events with signal words and dates.

How to Write Effective Paragraphs

Strategies	Applying the Strategies
• **Organize the paragraph around a main idea.**	• Begin most paragraphs with a topic sentence. Give details about the topic sentence in the other sentences of the paragraph.
• **Give information in a clear order, or sequence. Use transitions to lead from one sentence to the next.**	• Put ideas and events in an order that makes sense. Tie ideas together with transitions, such as *before*, *then*, *finally*, *in fact*, *another*, and *besides*.

Try This! In a science or social studies textbook, find a passage of at least three paragraphs on a topic that interests you. List the topic of the passage, the topic sentence of each paragraph, and the details that support each topic sentence.

Effective Paragraphs

Now it's your turn! Write a research report using effective paragraphs.

Writing Prompt

Research the history of your school or of another place in your town. Write a research report for your classmates.

Prewrite

Use an outline to plan your report.

Draft

Follow these steps:

STEP 1 **Introduce the topic.** Use your first paragraph to introduce your main topic.

STEP 2 **Write a topic sentence for your second paragraph.** Add supporting facts and details.

STEP 3 **Write a second topic sentence to start your third paragraph.** Add facts and details.

Strategies Good Writers Use

- Interview people who can give you information.
- Take clear notes. Put quotation marks around the exact words of speakers.
- Organize information by topics or time periods.

I. Introduction
II. Topic Sentence
    (main idea of
    paragraph)
    A. Detail
    B. Detail
III. Topic Sentence
    A. Detail
    B. Detail

Revise

Use this checklist to help you revise your report:

☑ Have you begun each paragraph after the first with a topic sentence?

☑ Do all the details in each paragraph tell about the main idea?

☑ Have you used transitions to tie sentences and paragraphs together?

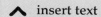

ℓ	delete text
∧	insert text
⟳	move text
¶	new paragraph
≡	capitalize
/	lowercase
○	correct spelling

Proofread

Use this checklist as you proofread:

☑ Have you used correct punctuation?

☑ Have you capitalized proper nouns?

☑ Did you check your spelling?

Publish and Reflect

Make a final copy of your research report, and share it with a partner. Tell what you like best about your partner's work. Discuss what each of you might do better next time. Write your ideas in your Writer's Journal.

Conventions

Written language follows certain **conventions,** or rules. We leave a space between words. We write in sentences that end with punctuation marks. Our readers understand these conventions.

When you proofread your writing, you check your use of English conventions. Here are some strategies to use as you proofread.

Proofreading Strategies

Wait before proofreading. It often helps to take a break after you write a draft. Then you can return to your work and look at it with a fresh eye.

Proofread in stages. You might want to follow these steps:

1. Read your writing and think about its meaning. Make sure your **sentences** are complete and make sense. Indent any **paragraphs.**

2. Now look at **grammar, usage, capitalization**, and **punctuation**. Do your sentences begin and end correctly? Do verbs agree with subjects? Have you used the correct forms of irregular verbs?

3. Last, look at **spelling**. Circle words that look wrong. Check them in a dictionary.

Proofread with a partner. A classmate may see errors you missed.

Proofreading Checklist

You can use this checklist as you proofread:

Sentences and Paragraphs

☑ Does every sentence have a subject and a predicate?
☑ Have I avoided run-on sentences?
☑ Have I used the correct end marks?
☑ Have I indented each paragraph?

Grammar and Usage

☑ Do my verbs agree with their subjects?
☑ Have I avoided mixing up verb tenses?
☑ Have I used the correct form of adjectives and adverbs that compare?

Capitalization and Punctuation

☑ Have I capitalized proper nouns and the pronoun *I*?
☑ Have I used commas to join the parts of a compound sentence?
☑ Have I used commas correctly in addresses, dates, and series of words?
☑ Have I used apostrophes correctly in possessive nouns and contractions?
☑ Have I used quotation marks correctly?

Spelling

☑ Am I sure of the spelling of every word?
☑ Have I always used the correct homophone?

Presenting Your Work

Once you have written, revised, and proofread your work, you still have one more decision to make. How will you publish, or share, your work? Will you write your final draft on paper? Will you make a video presentation?

Here are some ways to publish your writing. If you put your imagination to work, you can probably think of many more.

Strategies Good Writers Use

- Think about your audience. Should you publish in cursive or manuscript printing? Should you use large or small type?
- Consider whether illustrations or diagrams might make your ideas easier to understand.

Publishing Ideas for Any Type of Writing

- Read your writing aloud.

- Post it on a bulletin board.

- Attach it to an e-mail.

Publishing Ideas for Descriptive Writing

- Use art materials to make an illustrated brochure.

- Take or find photographs to illustrate the work and create a magazine article.

- Add sound effects and background music and make a tape recording.

- Make up a dance to go with your oral reading.

Publishing Ideas for Narrative Writing

- Turn your story into a play and perform it.

- Make an illustrated, covered book for the classroom library.

- Enter your story in a writing contest.

- Have volunteer performers act out your story.

Making a Video of a Story

STEP 1 Choose a story or a personal narrative you have written. Draw pictures showing the scenes in the story.

STEP 2 Attach the pictures in story order to a wall.

STEP 3 Decide whether you want to read your story or tell it. Practice the method you choose.

STEP 4 Use a video camera and cassette to shoot your video. Read or tell your story as the camera moves from picture to picture. If you are reading your story, you may want to have a partner shoot the video.

Publishing Ideas for Informational Writing

- Create a video presentation by reading your work in front of a video camera.

- Work with classmates to add illustrations and captions to informational articles and create a class magazine.

- Create a table display for the classroom or for a school fair.

- Combine news stories and create headlines to make a class newspaper.

- Make a poster for the school hallway.

- Take over as "teacher" and instruct your classmates.

Publishing Ideas for Persuasive Writing

- Send your work as a letter to the editor of your school or local paper.

- Give a speech to your class or at a school assembly.

- Present your ideas orally to a club or to the student council.

- Hold a classroom debate on the topic.

- Publish your work on your school's website.

Making an Oral Presentation

Strategies	Applying the Strategies
Make note cards.	Write each main idea on a note card. Include any major details. Write clearly and in large print.
Use visual aids.	Consider adding pictures, charts, diagrams, music, video, or electronic slides to make your presentation clearer and more interesting.
Practice.	Rehearse in front of a mirror, or present your talk to a friend or family member. Look for places where you might stress words or vary your rate or volume.
Present confidently.	Make eye contact with your audience. Use your note cards only as reference points. Speak loudly and clearly. Be prepared to answer questions from your audience.

Uppercase and Lowercase
Manuscript Alphabet

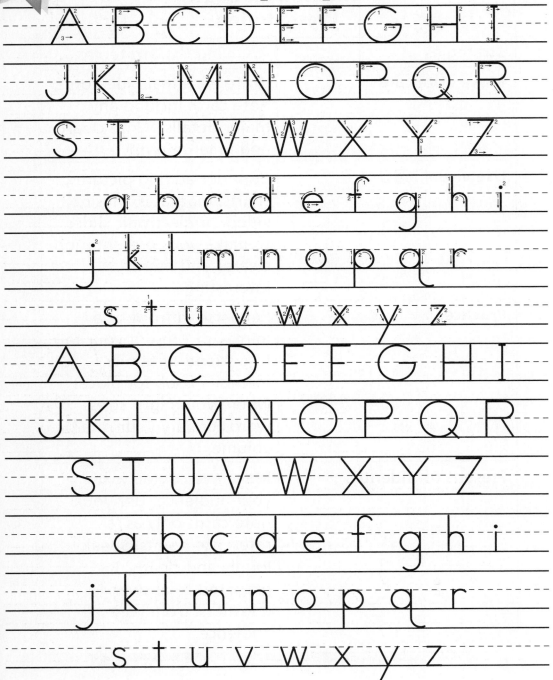

Uppercase and Lowercase
Cursive Alphabet

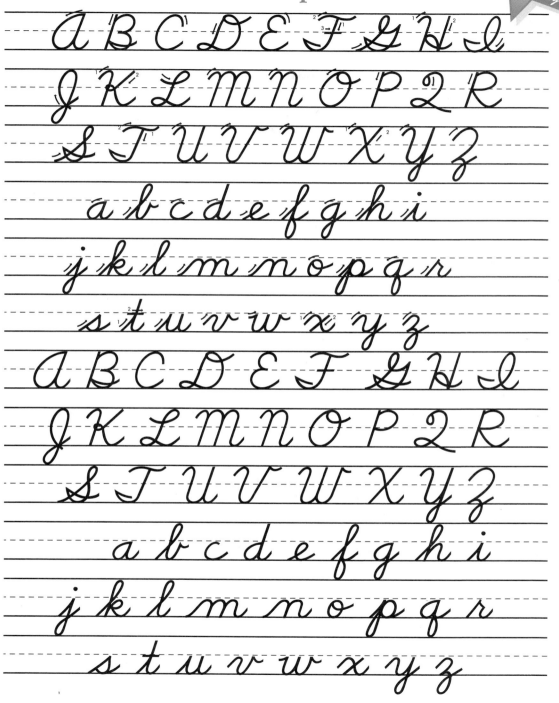

D'Nealian
Cursive Alphabet

A B C D E F G H

I J K L M N O P

2 R S T U V W

X Y Z

a b c d e f g h

i j k l m n

o p q r s t

u v w x y z

Elements of Handwriting

Shape

Write each letter using the correct shape.

correct

Friday

incorrect

Friday)

Spacing of Letters

Space letters properly so that they are easy to read.

not enough space between letters

house

correct spacing

house

too much space between letters

house

Spacing of Words and Sentences

This is a spacer: ☐. It is about the width of a pencil or pen. Leave room for one spacer between words and one spacer after end punctuation. Leave room for two spacers at the beginning of each paragraph.

Position

All letters should sit evenly on the bottom line.

correct

evenly

incorrect

evenly

Elements of Handwriting

Size

Tall letters fill one full space. Most short letters fill one half-space above the bottom line. Most tail letters fill one half-space above and one half-space below the bottom line.

correct

hobby

incorrect

hobby

Slant

Slant your letters in the same direction to make your writing easy to read.

correct

mark

incorrect

mark

Stroke

Keep your letter strokes smooth and steady. Do not mark over strokes you have already written. The letters should not be too light or too dark.

correct   **unsteady**   **too light**   **too dark**

eat   *eat*   *eat*   *eat*

Joining Letters

Use an overcurve stroke when you join another letter to a circle stroke letter. You will have to retrace the circle stroke.

ra ed ma ic ng

Look at the way these letters join with undercurve and overcurve letters.

undercurve   **overcurve**

sl fe tr   *un im*

Look at the way the uppercase letters **J**, **Y**, and **Z** join with lowercase letters.

undercurve   **overcurve**

Je Ye Ze   *Jo Ya*

Look at the way these letters join.

Ca Hi Ko Re Ur

Spelling Strategies

Maybe you are one of those lucky people who are naturally good at spelling. If not, you can learn to be a better speller. Here are some strategies that can help you study for a spelling test and create your own list of spelling words.

Learning to Spell a Word

Follow these steps to learn to spell a new word:

STEP 1 **Say the word.** Try to recall when you have heard the word used. Think about what it means.

STEP 2 **Look at the word.** Look for prefixes, suffixes, or other word parts you know. Think about other words that are related in meaning and spelling. Picture the word in your mind.

STEP 3 **Spell the word to yourself.** Think about the way each sound is spelled. Notice anything that is unusual about the spelling.

STEP 4 **Write the word while looking at it.** Check the way you have formed the letters. If you have not written the word clearly, write it again.

STEP 5 **Check your learning.** Cover the word and write it. If you did not spell the word correctly, go through these steps again.

Making a Personal Spelling List

You may want to set aside a few pages in your Writer's Journal for a personal spelling list. Here you can list words that you have misspelled and words that are tricky for you. Before you begin listing words, make columns on your pages for the letters of the alphabet. That way you can keep your words organized.

Follow these steps to make and use your spelling list.

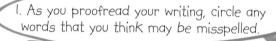

1. As you proofread your writing, circle any words that you think may be misspelled.

2. Find out how to spell the word correctly. Use a dictionary, or ask someone.

3. Write the word in your personal spelling list. Also write its meaning, or use it in a sentence.

4. Use your spelling list to check your spelling as you write and proofread.

Tips for Spotting Spelling Errors

- **Proofread your writing twice.** Read slowly and carefully to spot spelling errors.
- **Look at every letter.** Make your eyes go over every letter in every word.
- **Proofread backward.** You'll look at each word more carefully before moving on to the next word.

Peer Conferences

In a **peer conference,** two or more classmates come together to discuss and revise their writing. Hearing what your classmates have to say about your work can help you make it better.

Here are some strategies for getting the most out of a peer conference.

Strategies for Authors

Make copies of your work.
- If possible, give each person in the peer conference a copy.

Read the work aloud.
- You might read your work yourself, have someone else read your work aloud, or both. Hearing your work read aloud can help you recognize problems.

- If you read your own work, speak clearly. Match your voice to the ideas in the writing.

Listen and take notes.
- Jot down suggestions that classmates make about your writing.

- Be open to what your classmates tell you about your work. Try to understand their reasons. Think about ways to use their suggestions.

Strategies for Responders

Listen actively.
- Watch the speaker as the work is being read. Listen for the main idea, the supporting details, and the language used.

- Try to summarize the writing in your mind before you respond to it.

Make constructive comments.
- First, point out what you like. Then point out what is unclear or confusing.

- Be positive and polite. Remember that you are a writer, too. Always give ideas for improvement.

- Work together to get the best possible results.

Take notes.
- Jot down questions you want to ask the writer.

- Make notes about ideas that come to you as you listen to the work of others.

Keep an open mind.
- Don't judge writing by whether or not you agree with the writer's opinions.

Try This! Make a list of the Traits of Good Writing. After you read or listen to a classmate's work, put a checkmark beside each trait that you find in the work.

Using Rubrics

Have you ever wondered how your teacher grades writing assignments? Your teacher probably uses a kind of checklist or chart called a **rubric.**

Rubrics list traits to look for in writing. A paper that has all the traits earns the highest score. The highest score may be 4, 5, or 6.

You can use rubrics during writing to help you earn your highest score.

Before Writing

- Review the rubric to remind yourself of the traits of good writing.
- Keep these traits in mind as you prepare to write.

During Writing

- Check to see how well your draft matches the list of key traits.
- Put marks next to any trait that is missing from your draft.
- Use your marked rubric as you revise your draft.

After Writing

- Check your finished work against the rubric.
- If your work still can be improved, revise your writing again.

Strategies Good Writers Use

- Poor handwriting can make even good writing difficult to understand. Don't lose points because your writing can't be read.
- Remember that spelling counts! When in doubt, use a dictionary to check your spelling.

Some rubrics show only the highest score. Here is a sample rubric for a how-to essay. The highest score is 6 points.

SCORE OF 6 ★★★★★★

- The essay fits the purpose for writing. The audience it was written for would understand it. The topic is interesting.
- The essay has a clear beginning that introduces the topic, a middle that gives directions in a logical order, and an ending that summarizes or draws a conclusion.
- The essay uses signal words to help make the sequence of steps clear.
- The essay has description and details that add information about the directions.
- The essay has interesting words and phrases, especially specific nouns.
- The sentences are written in a variety of ways to make the writing interesting to read.
- The essay has few errors in spelling, grammar, and punctuation.

What other points do you think are important in a how-to essay?

Writing for Tests

Some kinds of tests ask for a written response to a writing **prompt**. The prompt tells you the topic of your writing assignment. It also tells you the purpose of your writing, and sometimes the audience. If the audience is not stated, write for an audience of your classmates and teacher.

Sample Writing Prompt

It's hard to be the "new kid" in a class, in a neighborhood, in a club, or on a team.

Before you begin writing, think of a time when you were the "new kid." Write a letter to a friend to tell about your experience.

This sentence introduces the topic.

This suggests ways to prewrite.

This tells you the type of writing—a friendly letter.

Analyzing Writing Prompts

Strategies	Applying the Strategies
Read the prompt carefully.	Read for a general sense of the topic and form.
Identify the topic, purpose, and form of your assignment.	Reread for clue words that tell you what you are supposed to do.
Restate your assignment.	Silently tell yourself in your own words what your assignment is.

Types of Writing Found on Tests

Type of Writing	Purpose	Clue Words in the Prompt
Narrative	to entertain, to tell a story	*write a story, tell about a time, tell what happened when*
Expository	to explain or define	*explain why, tell how, explain how you would*
Persuasive	to persuade or convince	*persuade, convince, tell why you think, explain why you would*
Summary	to inform by telling the main ideas in a piece of writing	*summarize, the most important ideas, in your own words*
Response to literature	to show your understanding of a selection	*explain, your response, what you learned*

Try This! Make up your own writing prompt. Exchange prompts with a partner, and analyze each other's prompt.

Managing Your Time

On standardized tests, you are told not only what you must write, but also how long you have to do it. Writing with a time limit can be tricky. You need to prewrite, draft, and edit your work in a short time. Learning to manage your time can help you succeed on writing tests.

These clocks show how you might divide your time for a 45-minute and for a 60-minute writing test.

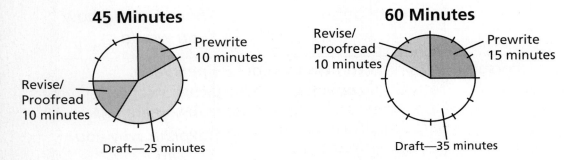

45 Minutes

Prewrite
10 minutes

Revise/
Proofread
10 minutes

Draft—25 minutes

60 Minutes

Revise/
Proofread
10 minutes

Prewrite
15 minutes

Draft—35 minutes

Strategies for Timed or Tested Writing

STEP 1 **Prewrite**
- Brainstorm ideas and choose a focus. Organize ideas in a list or graphic organizer.

STEP 2 **Draft**
- Use your prewriting notes to write a draft.
- Check to make sure you have done what the prompt asked you to do.

STEP 3 **Revise/Proofread**
- Add missing details.
- Take out details that don't fit.
- Check your grammar and spelling.

Writing Models

Story

In a **story,** a writer tells about one main idea. A story has *characters*, a *plot*, and a *setting*. The plot has a *beginning*, a *middle*, and an *ending*.

The Answering Machine with Wings

Mom and I were painting when the phone rang. I ran to answer it. It was Dad.

I put the receiver down on the table by the bird cage and went to get Mom. That's when Polly, our parrot, took over.

"Hello," said Polly. "Hi, honey. Okay. I love you. Bye-bye."

Mom grabbed the phone, but it was too late. Dad had hung up. Now we didn't know when or where his plane would land. Only Polly knew what Dad had said.

I suggested we call the airport, but Mom said we didn't know a flight number.

Then Polly squawked, "Okay, honey. Three o'clock, Gate 24."

Mom and I laughed. Soon we had a new answering machine—one with wings!

The title grabs the reader's attention.

beginning (with characters and setting)

middle (with problem)

Vivid verbs make writing more expressive.

ending (with problem solved)

Folktale

A **folktale** is a special story that was first told orally and has been passed from one storyteller to another. In many folktales, animals act like people.

The Lonely King's Friend

←title

Once there was a lonely king in India who kept canaries as pets. He loved to listen to their songs, but he was still lonely.

←beginning

←The opening paragraph sets up the problem.

One day the king's guards found a parrot and gave it to the king. When the canaries sang, the parrot screeched. The king put his hands over his ears.

←characters

"Oh, how can this be?" the king said loudly. "I want you to take away this awful bird!"

"Oh, how can this be?" answered the parrot loudly.

Now the king realized he had something special. He told his guards to leave the unusual bird.

←middle

"I haven't had a friend to talk to in a while," said the king.

"Oh, how can this be?" answered the bird.

"Well, let me tell you," said the king. The two of them talked for hours—and parrots have talked ever since.

←ending

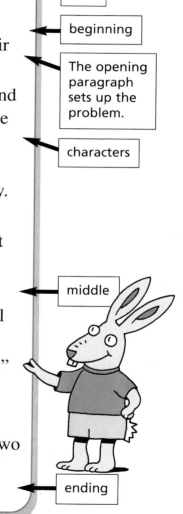

Character Sketch

In a **character sketch**, a writer describes a real or an imaginary person.

Amy Johnson in <u>The New Skates</u> is the youngest member of the Sport Barn's skating team. At four feet, two inches, she is a petite nine-year-old. However, what Amy lacks in size, she makes up in strength.

Amy began skating at the age of six. To keep up with her older brothers, she practices every day. Amy likes to skate for exercise and for fun. At age eight, she began practicing small turns in her basement when she couldn't skate outdoors.

When Amy first applied for a spot on the team, the store owners thought she was too young. Soon, Amy's skill, courage, and willingness not to give up changed the owners' minds. Amy is now the team's most valuable member.

topic sentence

how character looks and acts

Ideas are organized in time order.

what makes the character special

Descriptive Paragraph

A **descriptive paragraph** creates a word picture. It describes a person, a place, an object, or an event. It includes details that let the reader see, feel, hear, and sometimes taste and smell what is being described.

Morning Practice

The skater appeared out of the morning mist. Her strong body swayed from side to side. Her arms, legs, and long brown ponytail were swinging in time to the whoosh, whoosh of her skates on the hard road. As she came nearer, the still air stirred, bringing the aroma of breakfast muffins. Then, like a gust of wind, she passed by. I turned to watch as she vanished into the gray dawn.

title

topic sentence

Sensory details make the writing come alive.

Descriptive Essay

A **descriptive essay** creates a word picture as it tells about one subject. It has a beginning, a middle, and an ending. Like a descriptive paragraph, it includes sensory details.

The Contest

My older brothers and I have won several roller-skating contests. We practice for hours every weekend in Emerson Park. Last weekend, we were in our most unusual contest of all when we raced against nature.

When we walked into the park, the sun was bright and warm. My brothers and I laced up our skates and started down the narrow path. We skated in and out of patches of light and dark as we sped past huge oak trees. We stopped only once, to buy cool, refreshing cherry ice pops.

Halfway through the park and the ice pops, we felt a sudden chill. Gray clouds blocked the sun. Suddenly, the park was like a dark tunnel. The wind tossed twigs and acorns at our legs.

beginning that tells what you will describe

supporting paragraphs with sensory details

The writer uses details that appeal to the senses.

Thunder rumbled so loudly that it shook the ground. Beads of sweat dotted our foreheads as we skated faster, racing the oncoming storm. Our leg muscles burned. Our hearts pounded. At last, we saw the park exit.

We had won our race with the storm. We reached home just as the rain began. A flash of lightning reminded me of a camera flash going off to record our biggest race of all.

ending

Colorful words help readers to picture the scene.

Response to Literature

A **book review** is one kind of response to literature. It tells briefly what a book is about, without telling the ending. It also gives the writer's opinion of the book, explaining why others should or should not read it. The writer uses details from the book to support his or her opinion.

A response to literature might also be a response to an article, short story, or poem. Every time you write a response to literature, you should

- show that you understand the work.
- write about important elements such as characters, setting, plot, theme, and main idea.
- support your opinions and interpretations with facts and examples from the literature.

Grasshopper Summer

Grasshopper Summer by Ann Turner won several awards the year it was published. It tells the story of Sam White, an eleven-year-old boy, who moves from Kentucky to Dakota Territory in the year 1874. With his family, he settles a land that is barren and forbidding. Sam has a hard time adjusting to the move. He can't believe his brother Billy's opinion that everything will turn out fine.

title of the book

author's name

The main character is introduced.

The setting is described.

Even Billy's cheerfulness is challenged when the family's crops are wiped out by grasshoppers. How the family recovers from this terrible setback is a heartwarming, realistic story.

Historical fiction can sometimes seem dull, but this story is always exciting. Sam and Billy seem just like people you know, and that helps you imagine how you would feel in their place. I learned all about pioneers while reading this wonderful story about a tough, loving family. I would recommend this book to anyone who likes realistic fiction.

The turning point of the story is discussed.

The writer gives an opinion and supports it.

The writer tells whether others should read the book.

Summary

A **summary** is a brief statement of main points of something you have read or seen. A summary is written in the writer's own words. It contains only the main idea and a few important details. A summary helps the writer remember main points from source material such as films, observations, and printed materials.

Manatees

Manatees are large mammals also known as sea cows. They live only in water and can be found in the southeastern United States, South America, and Africa. They eat mostly water plants and can digest more than 100 pounds of plants each day. In some places in South America, they are used to keep waterways clean.

There are three species of manatees. The Caribbean manatee lives in salt or fresh water. This is the manatee that is found in the United States. It can grow up to 13 feet long and weigh close to 2 tons. The Amazon manatee lives only in the fresh water of the Amazon and Orinoco Rivers. The African manatee lives in the rivers and coastal waters of western Africa.

Although they are gentle beasts, all three species of manatee are endangered. They have been hunted in the past, and today their habitats are shrinking.

Article used as source material

first main idea

details

second main idea

details

third main idea

details

A manatee is a large water mammal that lives in fresh or salt water. There are three kinds of manatees. The Caribbean manatee lives in the southeastern United States and the Caribbean. The Amazon manatee lives in the rivers of South America. The African manatee lives in the rivers and ocean waters around western Africa. Manatees are endangered animals.

Summary includes main ideas and important details from source.

Personal Narrative

In a **personal narrative**, a writer tells about an experience in his or her life.

I never thought a homework assignment would make me famous at school, but it did. It began when my teacher, Mr. Reyes, asked us to write about a way we could help save the earth.

Once I had an idea about paper recycling, I wrote quickly. I shared my idea first with my class. Then I shared it with the whole school during assembly. Before I knew it, the Baxter plan was in use.

Each class now has boxes for white and colored paper. If only one side of a piece of paper has been used, it goes into a box. Other students then use the blank side for writing rough drafts, taking notes, or drawing and other art projects.

I'm proud to know I made a difference. I'm even prouder that my classmates helped me make that difference. You'd be amazed at how much paper we save!

strong beginning

middle that describes events in time order

The ending tells the importance of the experience.

Paragraph of Information

A **paragraph of information** gives facts about one topic.

title

Where Does All the Paper Go?

topic sentence

When paper is recycled, it doesn't just become recycled paper. It is made into many different new products. Some of these products include boxes for cereal and shoes. Recycled paper can also be used to make egg cartons, paper towels, and tissues. Some recycled paper helps people send messages to friends and family when it becomes greeting cards. Along with other resources, paper waste becomes plasterboard for the walls of homes and tar paper for under roofs. Even our cars may have paper waste in the form of stiffening for doors and sun visors.

Details all relate directly to the topic sentence.

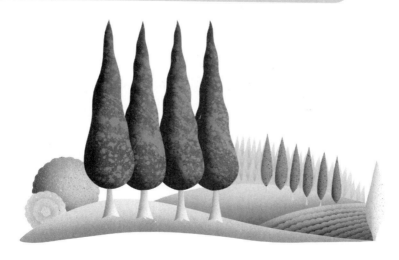

How-to Paragraph

A **how-to paragraph** gives directions or explains how to do something. Steps are given in time order.

How to Recycle Paper at Home

Help save trees by recycling paper at home. First, gather all your old and unwanted newspapers, magazines, and catalogs. Then separate the newspapers from glossy paper inserts. The inserts go with magazines and catalogs to be recycled. Next, place each kind of paper in a separate pile. When you have a bundle that is about 10 inches high, tie it up both lengthwise and around the middle with strong string. Finally, store your paper bundles in a dry place until recycling pickup day. If your community doesn't have a pickup, find out where you can take your paper to be recycled.

topic
sentence

materials
needed

Sequence
words put steps
in time order.

How-to Essay

A **how-to essay** explains in several paragraphs how to do something. It has a beginning, a middle, and an ending. It gives steps in time order.

Homemade Recycled Paper

Making your own recycled paper with an adult family member can be fun and will help save trees. You will need two newspaper pages, a large pan that is 3 inches deep, two pieces of window screen cut to fit the pan, a blender, and some water.

First, tear the newspaper into tiny pieces. Ask a family member to put the pieces in a blender, add 4 cups of water, place the lid on the blender, and turn it on. The thick mixture that forms is called pulp.

Next, put an inch of water in the pan. Place one screen in the pan and pour in the pulp. Then carefully lift the screen and shake it gently from side to side to even out the pulp and let the water drain.

Finally, place the second screen over the pulp, and squeeze to remove excess water. Set the screens and pulp aside to dry into your very own recycled paper.

topic sentence that tells what is being explained

materials needed

explanatory paragraphs in time order

Sequence words make the steps easy to follow.

Essay of Explanation

An **essay of explanation** is designed to inform. It explains a process or concept step by step. One good way to organize an explanatory essay is with an introduction, steps in order, and a conclusion.

How an Egg Becomes a Bird

Most wild birds lay eggs in spring. You have probably seen eggs in a nest. Did you ever wonder what was going on inside them?

Even before an egg is laid in the nest, cells are dividing inside it. The egg at this point has an outer layer and an inner layer. These are called the ectoderm and the endoderm.

The female bird then lays the egg. The parent birds sit on the egg to warm it. At the correct temperature, the two layers of the egg turn into three layers. The outer layer becomes the skin, feathers, and nervous system. The middle layer turns into bones, blood, and muscles. The inner layer becomes the respiratory and digestive systems. The growing bird embryo gets food from the egg yolk and air through the shell.

title

Introduction grabs the reader's attention.

beginning stage

Supporting details include definitions of unfamiliar terms.

middle stage

supporting details

After several weeks, the baby bird is ready to hatch. A careful listener will hear chirping, even before the eggshell cracks. A tapping sound means that the chick is pecking its way out. Finally the baby bird squeezes out of the shell, fully formed.

final stage

An egg is quite amazing. It looks very simple, but it contains everything the embryo needs to grow into a living, breathing bird.

Conclusion summarizes the main idea of the essay.

Essay of Comparison and Contrast

An **essay of comparison and contrast** shows how two or more things are alike and how they are different. It is organized in a way that emphasizes these likenesses and differences. For example, the first paragraph often introduces the two things that will be compared and contrasted. The next paragraph might tell how they are alike. The next paragraph might tell how they are different. Words such as *same, like, both, but, unlike,* and *however* may be used to signal comparison and contrast.

Two Kinds of Swallows

We have barn swallows and tree swallows on our farm. For a long time, I had trouble telling them apart, but now I know them by sight.

These two types of swallows are alike in many ways. Both are slim, graceful, blue-black birds with pointed wings and short bills. Both swoop around at dusk, catching insects on the fly.

The title tells the topic of the essay.

This paragraph tells how the two types of swallows are alike.

There are some differences, however. The barn swallow's tail is sharply divided into two points. It has an orange belly and white wing spots. The tree swallow has a shorter tail and a white belly. Unlike the barn swallow, the tree swallow swoops in circles, and it eats berries as well as insects. Their names hint at another difference. Barn swallows build nests inside barns, but tree swallows nest in holes in dead trees.

This paragraph tells how the two types of swallows are different.

Finally, I can tell these birds apart. When I see an insect-eating bird swoop by at dusk, I look at its tail and belly. I notice how it flies. I check what it eats and where it nests. Looking for these differences means that I will never mix up barn swallows and tree swallows again.

The conclusion tells how the information presented can be used.

Research Report and Outline

To write a **research report**, a writer gathers facts from different sources, takes notes, and makes an **outline**. The notes and outline are used to write about the topic. The sources are usually listed at the end of the report.

Outline

Outlines follow a certain form. Main ideas are shown with Roman numerals. Subtopics are shown with capital letters.

> ### From Used Paper to New
> I. Introduction
> II. How paper is recycled
>   A. Passing inspection
>   B. Forming the pulp
>   C. Changing the pulp into paper
> III. Conclusion

Research Report

A **research report** provides information about a topic. This short report follows the outline on page 74. Reports can be several pages long.

title

From Used Paper to New

In 1800, English inventor Matthias Koops found a way to make new paper from old paper. In the early 1900s, some paper mills in the United States began using his idea, but it took almost another hundred years for paper recycling to become popular.

Most paper mills now use his basic steps. First, the old paper is inspected for unwanted objects. Then it is cooked with hot water in a machine called a hydrapulper, which forms a pulp. The pulp goes through several washers and spinners to remove inks, dyes, and small objects. Next, it is fed onto wire mesh, where rollers press out the water. Heated rollers then iron the pulp smooth.

Although the idea of recycling paper is not new, people are just realizing its value now. Recycling paper offers an added bonus. It costs a lot less than making new paper.

introduction that identifies topic

body with information on subtopics

conclusion

The conclusion refers back to the main idea.

Persuasive Paragraph

In a **persuasive paragraph,** a writer tells his or her opinion about a topic. The writer tries to convince the audience to agree with the opinion and to take action.

I am strongly in favor of having small pets like rabbits at school. Animals are fun and educational to watch. Many kinds of pets are intelligent and can be trained to do things. Also, class members learn responsibility by having to take care of the pets' food and their homes. There are many small pets at the Nature Society that need good homes because they have been hurt or are unwanted. I think every class in this school should have a class pet!

opinion

The writer offers facts and reasons in support of his or her opinion.

restated opinion/request for action

Persuasive Essay

A **persuasive essay** has a beginning, a middle with paragraphs supporting the writer's opinion, and an ending.

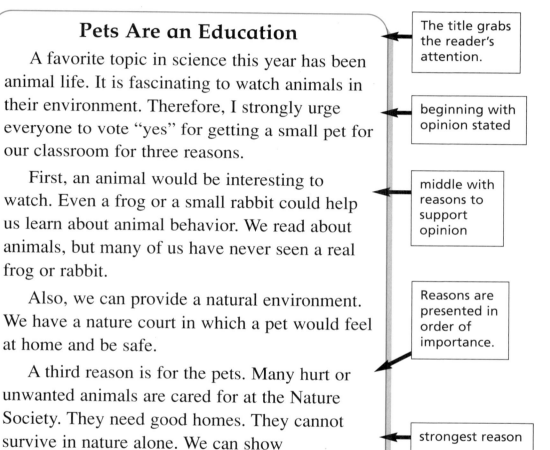

Pets Are an Education

A favorite topic in science this year has been animal life. It is fascinating to watch animals in their environment. Therefore, I strongly urge everyone to vote "yes" for getting a small pet for our classroom for three reasons.

First, an animal would be interesting to watch. Even a frog or a small rabbit could help us learn about animal behavior. We read about animals, but many of us have never seen a real frog or rabbit.

Also, we can provide a natural environment. We have a nature court in which a pet would feel at home and be safe.

A third reason is for the pets. Many hurt or unwanted animals are cared for at the Nature Society. They need good homes. They cannot survive in nature alone. We can show responsibility by adopting one of these animals.

Think of yourselves and the animals. Vote "yes" for a class pet!

The title grabs the reader's attention.

beginning with opinion stated

middle with reasons to support opinion

Reasons are presented in order of importance.

strongest reason

ending with restated opinion or request for action

Book Review

In a **book review**, a writer tells what a book is about without telling the whole story. The review also gives the writer's opinion of the book and suggests whether others should read it.

The Incredible Journey

The Incredible Journey by Sheila Burnford is an incredible book. It tells the story of a cat, Tao, and two dogs, Bodger and Luath, that set out across 250 miles of Canadian wilderness searching for their way home to the family they love.

When the adventure begins, the pets are staying with a friend while the family is away. Due to a mixup, the pets aren't missed for several weeks when they begin their journey. The pets are chased by wild animals, delayed by people, and challenged by nature.

You'll laugh and cry as you journey home with these three animals. They are courageous and true. This book is a must for animal lovers!

- title
- author
- main characters
- setting
- summary of book
- The writer concludes by encouraging the audience to read the book.

Television or Movie Review

In a **television** or **movie review**, a writer tells about a program or movie, gives an opinion on it, and says whether others should watch it.

Homeward Bound

<u>Homeward Bound</u> is a new movie based on Sheila Burnford's popular novel <u>The Incredible Journey</u>. It tells the story of a cat, Sassy, and two dogs, Chance and Shadow, that set out across the California wilderness to find their way home to the family they love.

This film closely follows the novel, with one major exception. In the movie, the animals have voices and talk. Some viewers will like this difference, but it may bother others. In either case, this is not a movie to be missed. The scenery is beautiful and the message of loyalty and love is great.

title

setting/main characters

why it should be seen

Friendly Letter

In a **friendly letter**, a person writes to someone he or she knows. A friendly letter has a *heading*, a *greeting*, a *body*, a *closing*, and a *signature*. In the heading, include a comma between the city and state and between the day of the month an

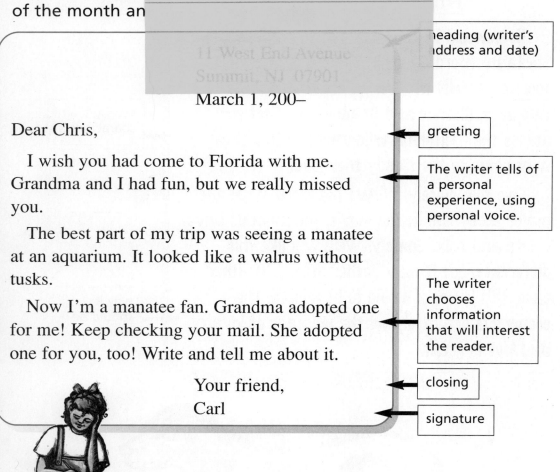

11 West End Avenue
Summit, NJ 07901

March 1, 200–

Dear Chris,

I wish you had come to Florida with me. Grandma and I had fun, but we really missed you.

The best part of my trip was seeing a manatee at an aquarium. It looked like a walrus without tusks.

Now I'm a manatee fan. Grandma adopted one for me! Keep checking your mail. She adopted one for you, too! Write and tell me about it.

Your friend,
Carl

heading (writer's address and date)

greeting

The writer tells of a personal experience, using personal voice.

The writer chooses information that will interest the reader.

closing

signature

Business Letter

A **business letter** can ask for or share information about business, order something, or praise or complain about a product or service. It uses formal language but has the same parts as a friendly letter, plus an **inside address**.

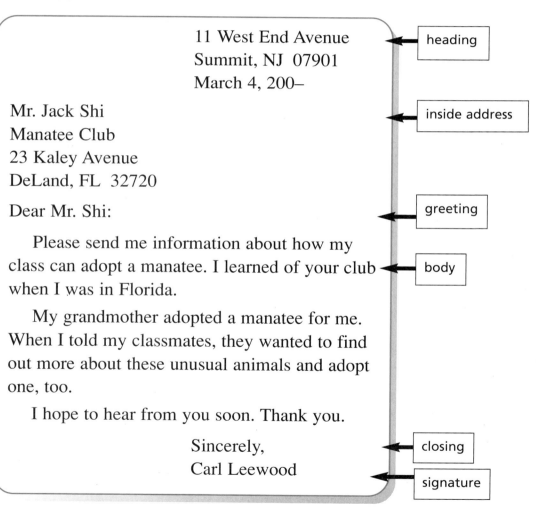

11 West End Avenue
Summit, NJ 07901
March 4, 200–
  → heading

Mr. Jack Shi
Manatee Club
23 Kaley Avenue
DeLand, FL 32720
  → inside address

Dear Mr. Shi:
  → greeting

Please send me information about how my class can adopt a manatee. I learned of your club when I was in Florida.
  → body

My grandmother adopted a manatee for me. When I told my classmates, they wanted to find out more about these unusual animals and adopt one, too.

I hope to hear from you soon. Thank you.

Sincerely,
  → closing
Carl Leewood
  → signature

Envelope

A letter is sent in an **envelope** that shows the *receiver's address* and *return address*. A *postal abbreviation* for each state and a *ZIP code* are included.

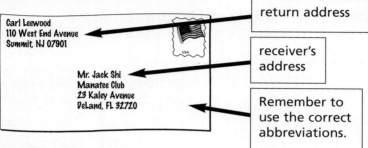

return address

receiver's address

Remember to use the correct abbreviations.

Carl Leewood
110 West End Avenue
Summit, NJ 07901

Mr. Jack Shi
Manatee Club
23 Kaley Avenue
DeLand, FL 32720

Postal Abbreviations

Alabama AL	Kentucky KY	Ohio OH
Alaska AK	Louisiana LA	Oklahoma OK
Arizona AZ	Maine ME	Oregon OR
Arkansas AR	Maryland MD	Pennsylvania PA
California CA	Massachusetts MA	Rhode Island RI
Colorado CO	Michigan MI	South Carolina SC
Connecticut CT	Minnesota MN	South Dakota SD
Delaware DE	Mississippi MS	Tennessee TN
District of	Missouri MO	Texas TX
Columbia DC	Montana MT	Utah UT
Florida FL	Nebraska NE	Vermont VT
Georgia GA	Nevada NV	Virginia VA
Hawaii HI	New Hampshire NH	Washington WA
Idaho ID	New Jersey NJ	West Virginia WV
Illinois IL	New Mexico NM	Wisconsin WI
Indiana IN	New York NY	Wyoming WY
Iowa IA	North Carolina NC	
Kansas KS	North Dakota ND	

Message

A **message** states information received in person or by telephone. It tells whom the message is for and what it is about. It also tells the date and time of the message and the name of the person taking the message. Ask the person leaving the message to spell or repeat anything that is unclear.

Saturday
11:30 a.m.

Carl,

Mrs. Cassidy called. The information on the class manatee, Sebastian, has arrived. Call her at the school at 555-4215 before 1 p.m. if you want to see it.

Pat

- day and time
- name of person message is for
- name of caller
- message
- telephone number of caller
- recorder's name

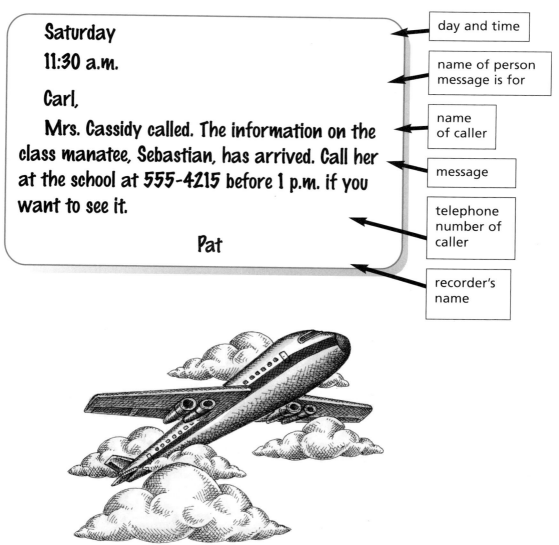

Form

A **form** is a sheet of paper with blanks used to write in information. Some of the reasons you fill out forms are to apply for a job, enter a contest, order from a catalog, or join a club.

Tips for Filling Out Forms

• Read the *whole form* before you begin to write.

• Be alert for directions that tell you to use pencil or pen.

• Check carefully to see where you should write. The line on which your name should appear, for example, may not be right next to the word *Name*. Instead, it may be below or above it.

• Watch for directions that tell you to print instead of write. Always print or write neatly.

• Give all the information you are asked for. When you are finished, look over the form to be sure you have completed it correctly.

• Turn the form over to see if there are questions on both sides.

This is a form for a club. Note the directions at the beginning of the form.

Save the Manatee Club

Please print in ink.

Name ___Leewood_____Carl_____
          (last)   (first)

Address _____11 West End Avenue_____
                    (Number and Street)

___Summit_____NJ_____07091_____
    (City)   (State)   (Zip)

Tel.# ___(212) 555-2801_____ Age __9____

Grade ___4_____ Teacher ___Mrs. Cassidy___

School Name ___Harris Elementary_____

Address _____401 McLeod Avenue_____
                    (Number and Street)

___Summit_____NJ_____07091_____
    (City)   (State)   (Zip)

Where did you learn about our club?

_____an aquarium in Florida_____

I want information about a manatee for:

_____ myself   ___X___ my class

Notes and Questionnaire

Notes are written records that help you remember information. You take notes in class to help you remember what you hear or read. You also take notes to write a research report or to study for a test.

One of the best ways to take notes for a report or test is to use index cards. Use one card for each main idea. Add facts to the card.

topic

Manatee Dangers

How do people endanger manatees?
- manatees hurt by boat propellers
- pollution destroys feeding areas

Endangered Wildlife by Adam Kroll, p. 98

main idea as question

facts in your own words

source (book, author, page number)

A **questionnaire** is a written list of questions used to get information. The results can be used in experiments, reports, and speeches.

Survey on Endangered Animals

1. Which of these animals have you heard of? Check all that apply.

_____ Caribbean manatee

_____ Black-footed ferret

_____ Whooping crane

_____ California condor

_____ Hawaiian monk seal

_____ Desert tortoise

_____ Right whale

_____ Florida panther

2. In your opinion, what is the main reason animals become endangered?

_____

3. Please tell a bit about yourself by circling the answer to each question.

Which are you?   a boy   a girl

What grade are you in?   3   4   5   6

Does your family have a pet?   yes   no

Title tells topic of questionnaire.

includes question(s) to find out about prior knowledge of the topic

includes question(s) to find out about opinions

includes question(s) to find out about person answering questionnaire

Charts and Diagrams

A **chart** is a visual way of showing a lot of information. Charts are set up in rows and columns. To find the information you need, you read across rows and down columns. Titles and headings help you locate information on charts. Most word processing programs include easy ways to create professional-looking charts. When you create a chart, the following tips will be helpful.

- Gather all the information you want to include first.
- Think about the best way to organize the information.
- Organize your chart in rows and columns with headings.
- Give your chart a title so the reader knows what it is about.

Animal Names			
Animal	Male	Female	Young
bear	boar	sow	cub
deer	buck	doe	fawn
fox	dog	vixen	cub
rabbit	buck	doe	bunny
turkey	tom	hen	poult

Largest Animals		
Animal	Length	Weight
MAMMAL Blue Whale	100 ft.	150 tons
AMPHIBIAN Giant Salamander	5 ft.	100 lb.
REPTILE Saltwater Crocodile	16 ft.	1/2 ton
BIRD Condor	15 ft.	25 lb.
FISH Whale Shark	45 ft.	13 tons

A **diagram** is a visual way of organizing information. Usually a diagram uses graphics and words to classify or categorize.

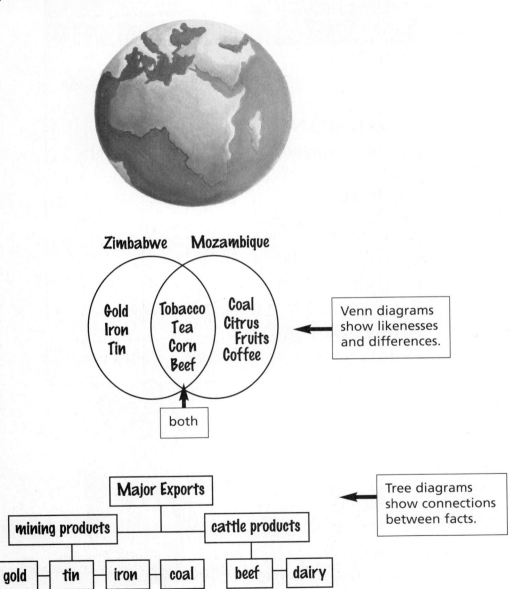

Zimbabwe   Mozambique

Gold   Tobacco   Coal
Iron   Tea   Citrus
Tin   Corn   Fruits
        Beef   Coffee

Venn diagrams show likenesses and differences.

both

Major Exports

mining products   cattle products

gold   tin   iron   coal   beef   dairy

Tree diagrams show connections between facts.

Grammar, Usage, and Mechanics

SENTENCES

- A **sentence** is a group of words that tells a complete thought.

- A sentence names someone or something. It tells what that person or thing is or does.

- The words in a sentence are in an order that makes sense.

- A sentence begins with a capital letter and ends with an end mark.

If the words form a sentence, write *sentence.* If not, think of words to make the sentence complete. Write the new sentence.

1. **Found a secret place.**

2. **She planted a roof garden.**

3. **The blooming flowers.**

4. **The smell of the flowers.**

Rewrite these sentences, putting the words in an order that makes sense.

5. **loves Grandma gardens.**

6. **I the believed story.**

7. **seemed Lydia Grace real.**

8. **see did you plants the lovely?**

SENTENCES

Write each sentence. Use proofreading marks to add a capital letter and an end mark to each sentence.

1. **she was far from home**

2. **she was lonely**

3. **her uncle seemed gloomy**

4. **how could she cheer him up**

Write Lydia Grace's letter, making each sentence complete. Add capital letters and end marks where they are needed.

Dear Grandma,

I discovered a secret place on the roof. no one else knows about it Only the cat and I have been there. I have plans. To make the place beautiful. i think Uncle Jim will finally smile I wish you could see it.

Love,

Lydia Grace

CUMULATIVE REVIEW

Think of words to turn these word groups into complete sentences. Write the sentences.

1. sweet-smelling rolls
2. after I swept the floor
3. decorated a cake
4. made cookies
5. many new customers
6. bought pies and cookies

Write the following sentences, putting the words in an order that makes sense. Use correct capitalization.

7. Emma a cookies box with filled.
8. A bow tied around it she.
9. The her customer a gave dollar.
10. Took he the cookies.

DECLARATIVE AND INTERROGATIVE SENTENCES

- A **declarative sentence** tells something. It ends with a period.
- An **interrogative sentence** asks a question. It ends with a question mark.

Write whether each sentence is *declarative* or *interrogative.*

1. **Donavan used the dictionary.**
2. **Why did he need it?**
3. **Was he looking up a word?**
4. **New words are his passion.**
5. **Maybe he will be a poet.**

Write each sentence, adding the correct end mark.

6. **Does Donavan write well**
7. **His teacher likes his work**
8. **Have you read his stories**
9. **He wrote one about his grandmother**
10. **She led an interesting life**

11.–12. Write one question you would like to ask your favorite writer. Then write one declarative sentence about that writer's work. Begin and end your sentences correctly.

DECLARATIVE AND INTERROGATIVE SENTENCES

Write each sentence, using a capital letter and the correct end mark. Then identify each sentence as *declarative* or *interrogative.*

1. who took all the words

2. the words made everyone feel better

3. how many words does Donavan have now

4. will Miss Millie talk to people more often

5. mr. Kincaid will stop working so hard

6. grandma's neighbors were never so lively before

7. donavan doesn't want his words back

8. do any of those words describe you

9.–10. Write one declarative sentence and one interrogative sentence of your own about Donavan's words.

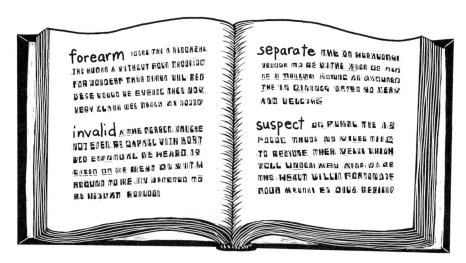

CUMULATIVE REVIEW

Think of words to turn these word groups into complete sentences. Write the sentences.

1. after I left
2. walked to the store
3. several neighbors
4. sat on the front steps
5. some neighborhood boys

Write each sentence. Use the correct capital letter and end mark.

6. will you come to dinner tonight
7. dad is a very good cook
8. we had soup and crackers for lunch
9. was it tomato soup or chowder
10. the crackers were delicious

IMPERATIVE AND EXCLAMATORY SENTENCES

- An **imperative sentence** gives a command. It ends with a period.

- An **exclamatory sentence** shows strong feeling. It ends with an exclamation point.

Write whether each sentence is *imperative* or *exclamatory*.

1. Teach María the song.

2. Wow, she sings it well!

3. How quickly she learned it!

4. Please play it on the piano.

5. What a low note you hit!

Write each sentence. Add the correct end mark.

6. Stand in the center of the stage

7. I can't believe how many people are here

8. Please don't be nervous

9. You performed so well

10.–11. Write one imperative sentence and one exclamatory sentence about a time you were part of a performance. Be sure to use the correct end marks.

IMPERATIVE AND EXCLAMATORY SENTENCES

1.–8. María Isabel's parents loved the show. Write their remarks, adding the correct end mark to each. Then identify their remarks as *imperative* or *exclamatory*.

Mr. Salazar

Come here, Chabelita

Wow, the acting was so good

Give Papi a hug

How proud I am

Mrs. Salazar

What a nice pageant it was

Please introduce us to your teacher

How well you sang

Tell us about the song

CUMULATIVE REVIEW

Choose the best way to write each underlined section.

Mr. Salazar gave his daughter two barrettes. (1) <u>How beautiful they were?</u> She wore them (2) <u>in the school pageant. They twinkled</u> in the lights. Look at (3) <u>this picture doesn't she</u> look wonderful? (4) <u>Will she wear them again at graduation</u>.

1. They were how beautiful.

   How beautiful they were!

   How beautiful! They were.

   No mistake

2. in the school pageant, they twinkled

   in the school pageant they twinkled

   in the school pageant? They twinkled

   No mistake

3. this picture, doesn't she

   this picture. Doesn't she

   this picture? Doesn't she

   No mistake

4. Will she wear them. Again at graduation.

   Will she wear them again at graduation!

   Will she wear them again at graduation?

   No mistake

SUBJECTS AND PREDICATES

Write the subject to tell who or what the sentence is about.

1. **Lou Gehrig catches the ball.**

2. **He throws it to third base.**

3. **Everyone cheers loudly.**

4. **The players tip their hats.**

Write the predicate to tell what the subject is or does.

5. **The Yankees win the game.**

6. **Their fans go wild.**

7. **They run onto the field.**

8. **Everybody is excited.**

9.–11. Write three statements about a person or several people you admire. Draw one line under the subject and two lines under the predicate of each sentence you write.

SUBJECTS AND PREDICATES

Read this sportswriter's report about a 1931 Yankee game. Identify the subject and predicate of each sentence.

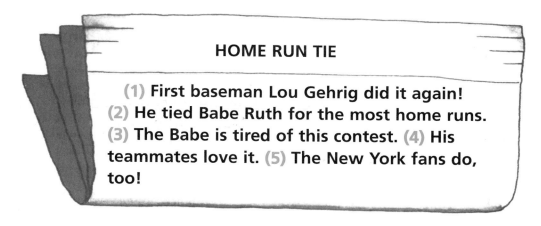

HOME RUN TIE

(1) First baseman Lou Gehrig did it again! (2) He tied Babe Ruth for the most home runs. (3) The Babe is tired of this contest. (4) His teammates love it. (5) The New York fans do, too!

Help the sportswriter complete each sentence. Add a subject or a predicate.

6. Most baseball players ____ .

7. Lou Gehrig ____ .

8. ____ watched Friday's game.

9. ____ enjoyed every minute.

10. That Yankee team ____ .

CUMULATIVE REVIEW

Write each sentence, using a capital letter and an end mark.
Then identify the sentence as *declarative, interrogative,
imperative,* or *exclamatory.*

1. we played baseball Saturday
2. what a great time we had
3. did your team win
4. watch us play sometime
5. that pitcher is so good
6. have you played the Tigers
7. we play them next week
8. please come to the game

Identify the subject and the predicate of each sentence.

9. Sandra tries on her uniform.
10. The red buttons look nice.
11. She likes the team's name very much.
12. The name of her team is "The Danby Dragons."

COMPLETE AND SIMPLE SUBJECTS

- The **complete subject** tells who or what the sentence is about.
- The **simple subject** is the main word or words in the complete subject.

Write the complete subject of each sentence. Then write the simple subject.

1. **The blizzard struck suddenly.**
2. **The sky was dark and gray.**
3. **A strong wind blew fiercely.**
4. **Laura's hands nearly froze.**
5. **Her red mittens hardly helped.**
6. **Snow piled up quickly.**

7.–11. Use the subjects and predicates in the box below to write sentences that make sense. Underline the simple subject of each sentence.

The wind	**growled nervously.**
The little dog	**filled the woodbox.**
Laura	**was colder than icicles.**
Many logs	**ran to the woodpile.**
The girls' parents	**felt proud of them.**

COMPLETE AND SIMPLE SUBJECTS

Laura wrote a short paragraph about a snowstorm. Write the complete subject and the simple subject of each sentence.

(1) **My sisters are very brave.** (2) **They helped our family in a snowstorm.** (3) **Our woodbox was empty.** (4) **We filled it without any help from our parents.** (5) **The little house stayed warm and cozy.**

Think of ways your family members have helped each other recently. Write each predicate, adding a complete subject to make a sentence. Circle the simple subject.

6. **cooked great meals.**

7. **did the laundry.**

8. **worked hard every day.**

9. **helped me with homework.**

10. **cleaned my room.**

Use each group of words as the complete subject of a sentence. Write the sentence.

11. **The food on the stove**

12. **My homework**

CUMULATIVE REVIEW

Identify the subject and the predicate of each sentence.

1. I have two sisters, a mother, and a father.
2. We live in a log cabin.
3. It is very cozy.
4. The oldest girl in my family is Mary.
5. Carrie is the youngest girl in my family.
6. She needs my help quite often.
7. She had a birthday just last month.
8. Her favorite toy is a rag doll.
9. Our dog's name is Jack.

Think of a complete subject for each predicate. Then write each sentence. Circle the simple subject in each sentence.

10. tells about pioneer life.
11. had few toys.
12. played with her sisters.
13. played outdoors.
14. helped with chores.
15. was cold.
16. made a snowman.

COMPLETE AND SIMPLE PREDICATES

Write the complete predicate of each sentence. Then write the simple predicate.

1. **The farmer's children argued too much.**
2. **His wife disliked the fighting.**
3. **The couple thought of a plan.**
4. **They sent the children away.**
5. **The children solved the problem.**

Look at the subjects and predicates listed below. Match each subject with a predicate to create a sentence that makes sense. Write each sentence, and underline the simple predicate.

SUBJECTS	PREDICATES
The sun	opened her bundle.
The oldest girl	set behind the hills.
Two stones	returned home safely.
A canteen	lay in the bundle.
The children	held water.

COMPLETE AND SIMPLE PREDICATES

The seven children wrote about their adventure. Write the complete predicate of each sentence. Then write the simple predicate.

(1) **The children in our family lost their way.** (2) **We argued at first.** (3) **All of us worked together.** (4) **We learned an important lesson.** (5) **You succeed better with friends.**

Add a complete predicate to each subject. Circle the simple predicate in each sentence you write.

6. **Hard work**
7. **A smile**
8. **Polite behavior**
9. **Good table manners**
10. **Honesty**
11. **Families**

CUMULATIVE REVIEW

Write each sentence. Draw one line under the complete subject.
Draw two lines under the complete predicate.

1. **The youngest boy cried.**
2. **The oldest girl hugged him.**
3. **The other children sat on the ground.**
4. **They waited for sunrise.**
5. **The sun peeked out of a cloud.**
6. **The children felt strong and happy.**

Write a complete subject for each predicate. Write a complete predicate for each subject. Then draw one line under each simple subject and two lines under each simple predicate.

7. **The seven children**
8. **Their mother**
9. **taught the children a good lesson.**
10. **never fought again.**
11. **The whole family**
12. **were pleased to see their children.**

COMPOUND SUBJECTS AND PREDICATES

- A **compound subject** is two or more subjects that share a predicate. A **compound predicate** is two or more predicates that share a subject.
- If there are three or more subjects or predicates in a sentence, use commas to separate them.

Read each sentence. Write the simple subject of each compound subject. Include the word that connects the subjects (*and* or *or*).

Example: The house and the barn burned down. house and barn

1. **The garden and the wall look beautiful now.**
2. **The children and their parents love the garden.**
3. **Bugs, rain, or rabbits are no problem.**
4. **Pests and bad weather do not worry us.**

Read each sentence. Write the simple predicate of each compound predicate. Include the word that connects the predicates (*and* or *or*).

Example: Mother held the cat and petted the dog. held and petted

5. **We cleared a vacant lot and built a garden.**
6. **The work took a lot of time and raised many blisters.**
7. **The neighbors tilled the ground or sowed seeds.**
8. **Children watched from their stoops or joined in.**

COMPOUND SUBJECTS AND PREDICATES

Rewrite each sentence. Add commas where they are needed.

1. **The teenagers prepare clean and paint the wall.**

2. **Flowers birds or leaves flow from their brushes.**

Each pair of sentences has the same predicate but different subjects. Rewrite each pair as one sentence with a compound subject, using *and* or *or*.

3. **The girl planted seeds. Her neighbors planted seeds.**

4. **The tomatoes will sprout first. The beans will sprout first.**

5. **The watering can came in handy. The spade came in handy.**

Each group of sentences has the same subject but different predicates. Rewrite each group as one sentence with a compound predicate, using *and* or *or.*

6. **We can pick the tomato. We can leave it to ripen another day.**

7. **Marisol brought a watering can. Marisol watered her seeds.**

8. **Marisol's plant sprouted. Marisol's plant grew very tall. Marisol's plant blossomed into a beautiful sunflower.**

CUMULATIVE REVIEW

Write each sentence. Draw one line under each complete subject and two lines under each complete predicate. Then write whether each sentence has a *compound subject* or a *compound predicate*.

1. The sunflower bobbed and nodded.
2. Marisol and Juan watered it.
3. Some neighbors picked and ate fruit.
4. They tasted apples or set them aside.
5. The sun or the rain fed the plants.

Read each sentence. Write the simple subject or predicate. Include the word that connects the compound subjects or compound predicates (*and* or *or*).

6. Mr. Castro and Marisol watered their seedlings.
7. Marisol's neighbor leaned on her shovel and wiped her forehead.
8. The petals curled and faded.

Write each sentence, adding commas where they are needed.

9. Sunflowers pansies and roses bloom.
10. Birds butterflies or bees suck nectar.
11. The flowers bloom quickly wither slowly and droop.

SIMPLE AND COMPOUND SENTENCES

Skill Reminder

- A **compound sentence** is made up of two or more simple sentences. They may be joined with the conjunctions *and, or,* or *but.*

- Use a comma before a conjunction that joins two sentences.

Identify each word group as a *comma splice* or a *run-on sentence.* Then write each sentence correctly as a compound sentence.

1. **We never see the pufflings, their parents do.**

2. **One puffin swoops down it catches a fish.**

Write each pair of sentences as a compound sentence, using the conjunction in parentheses ( ).

3. **Pufflings eat a lot. They keep their parents busy. (and)**

4. **Young puffins stay close to shore. The older birds fly out to sea. (but)**

5. **They have to peep loudly. Their parents won't hear them. (or)**

6. **The puffins dive. They emerge with fish. (and)**

SIMPLE AND COMPOUND SENTENCES

Halla wrote a report about puffins. Write each pair of sentences as a compound sentence, using *and, or,* or *but.*

1. The puffins live in burrows. The burrows protect them.
2. The puffins build nests. The nests protect their eggs.
3. We can hear the babies peep for food. We never see them.
4. The puffins are usually flying. They are diving for fish.

Write each sentence, placing commas where they are needed.

5. One puffling runs in front of Halla and she grabs it.
6. Halla meets her friends and they hike down to the beach.
7. The wind is strong and the air is cool.
8. Halla zips her jacket and she pulls her hat over her ears.
9. The pufflings are ready to fly and they flap their wings.
10. The children watch them fly away and Halla smiles.

CUMULATIVE REVIEW

Tell whether each sentence has a *compound subject,* has a *compound predicate,* or is a *compound sentence.* Then write the conjunction.

1. **Puffins and gulls are sea birds.**
2. **They swim and dive well.**
3. **They eat fish, or they eat scraps.**
4. **Gulls fly well, but puffins do not.**
5. **They wobble or drop like a stone.**
6. **Halla and her friends rescue the pufflings.**

Write each pair of sentences as a compound sentence, using the conjunction in parentheses ( ).

7. **Puffins look like penguins. They are quite different. (but)**
8. **Both live in cold water. Both eat fish. (and)**
9. **Penguins can swim. They can walk awkwardly. (or)**
10. **Puffins spend the winter at sea. They come ashore to lay their eggs. (but)**

CLAUSES

Write each sentence. Draw one line under each independent clause. Draw two lines under each dependent clause.

1. When the spider web was finished, it said "Some Pig."

2. Because Wilbur is a pig, he eats a lot.

3. Charlotte was tired after she completed the web.

4. Since the words were clear, Lurvy was amazed.

5. After he read the web, he ran out quickly.

6. He was afraid because it seemed so strange.

7.–8. Write two new sentences, using the following independent clause. Add a different dependent clause for each sentence.

Charlotte spun a web.

CLAUSES

Write each sentence. Draw one line under each independent clause. Draw two lines under each dependent clause.

1. We love our pig because he is sweet.
2. When Wilbur talks, the farmyard listens.
3. Before Charlotte spun the words in the web, Wilbur was in danger.
4. After Wilbur escaped, the geese caught him.
5. Everyone is happier when Wilbur is happy.

Write each group of words, adding the type of clause shown in parentheses ( ) to make a complete sentence. Remember to add commas as needed.

6. after he meets Charlotte (independent)
7. he is a good friend (dependent)
8. Wilbur is helpful (dependent)
9. because he is a cute pig (independent)
10. I love that pig (dependent)

CUMULATIVE REVIEW

Write each sentence. Underline the independent clauses, and circle the conjunction that connects them.

1. Charlotte is a spider, and Wilbur is a pig.
2. They live peacefully, but they are in danger.
3. Avery wants Charlotte, but Fern saves her.
4. Wilbur will be killed, or Charlotte will rescue him.
5. The two are friends, and they like each other.

Write each group of words, adding the type of clause shown in parentheses ( ) to make a complete sentence. Remember to add commas as needed.

6. because Wilbur is frightened (independent)
7. Wilbur may be eaten (dependent)
8. Charlotte has an idea (dependent)
9. since Charlotte is very smart (independent)
10. Wilbur is saved (dependent)

COMPLEX SENTENCES

Skill Reminder

- A **complex sentence** is made up of an independent clause and at least one dependent clause.

Tell whether each sentence is *simple*, *compound*, or *complex*.

1. **Orangutans live in the rain forest.**

2. **Since baby orangutans are cute, animal dealers want them.**

3. **I love the babies, but they grow up fast.**

4. **When they grow up, they need less care.**

Write each sentence. Draw one line under each independent clause and two lines under each dependent clause.

5. **I wear a hat when it rains each afternoon.**

6. **Since the babies make leaf hats, they keep quite dry.**

7. **Because it is so wet, we hide under trees.**

Make a complex sentence from each sentence pair. Write each sentence, using commas where they are needed.

8. **It rains. We run for shelter.**

9. **The rain will not soak us. We hide.**

10. **I have a hat. My hair still gets wet.**

COMPLEX SENTENCES

One baby-sitter made notes about the orangutans. Combine each pair of sentences into a complex sentence. The connecting words in the box may help you.

after	because	since	when
although	before	if	while

1. **Nanang bites the washcloth. He hates water.**

2. **Nanang has a bath. He climbs to the top of the tree.**

3. **His hand seems sore. Nanang climbs well.**

4. **He hides in a tree. It is bedtime.**

5. **Nanang will come to bed. I offer him a snack.**

6.–10. For each complex sentence you wrote, underline the independent clause once and the dependent clause twice.

CUMULATIVE REVIEW

Choose the best way to write each underlined sentence.

(1) **When baby orangutans lose their mothers they need baby-sitters.** (2) **I am one of those baby-sitters.** (3) **Nanang is my favorite but I love the others, too.** (4) **Although I'll eat bananas for Nanang, I won't eat termites.**

1. When baby orangutans need mothers.

   Baby orangutans lose their mothers they need baby-sitters

   When baby orangutans lose their mothers, they need baby-sitters.

   No mistake

2. I, am one of those baby-sitters.

   Me one of those baby-sitters

   A baby-sitter I am.

   No mistake

3. Nanang is my favorite but the others I love too.

   Nanang is my favorite, but I love the others, too.

   Nanang is my favorite I love the others too

   No mistake

4. Although I'll eat bananas. I won't eat termites.

   Although Nanang won't eat bananas I will.

   I'll eat bananas for Nanang, I won't eat termites.

   No mistake

COMMON AND PROPER NOUNS

- A **noun** is a word that names a person, a place, a thing, or an idea.
- A **common noun** names any person, place, thing, or idea.
- A **proper noun** names a particular person, place, thing, or idea.

Write the nouns from each sentence. Then write *C* for a common noun and *P* for a proper noun.

1. Jack was a wonderful horse.
2. Anna and Caleb hoped Sarah would stay.
3. Could the woman carry the sea to the countryside?
4. Sarah brought gifts from Maine.
5. The family enjoyed the stew and the bread.

Write the sentences, replacing underlined common nouns with proper nouns and underlined proper nouns with common nouns.

6. Sarah rested after her long trip.
7. The family traveled to the town.
8. Thanksgiving Day is in November.
9. After dinner, the children washed the dishes.

COMMON AND PROPER NOUNS

Write each sentence, adding a noun that tells about the picture. Use the kind of noun shown in parentheses ( ).

1. **These are (common).**

2. **This is a (common).**

3. **Anna and Caleb call me (proper).**

4. **I am a (common).**

5. **My name is (proper).**

6. **I am Caleb's (common).**

7. **Hi! I'm (proper).**

8. **I'm Papa's (common).**

9. **My name is (proper).**

10. **I am a (common).**

11. **This is (proper).**

12. **She is Sarah's (common).**

13. **These animals are named (proper) and (proper).**

14. **They are (common).**

REVIEW

Write each sentence, using the correct end mark. Then write whether each sentence is *declarative* or *interrogative.*

1. Do you like my bonnet, Anna
2. Here are some gifts for you
3. You can hear the sea in this shell
4. Is anyone hungry yet

Write each sentence. Draw one line under each independent clause and two lines under each dependent clause. Then write whether each sentence is simple or complex.

5. Sarah drew pictures of the farm while we watched.
6. Will her brother enjoy the pictures?
7. Papa showed Sarah a dune made of hay.
8. When Sarah touched the sheep, she smiled.

For each proper noun, write a common noun. For each common noun, write a proper noun.

9. teacher
10. Rio Grande
11. mountain
12. July

SINGULAR AND PLURAL NOUNS

- Form the plural of most nouns by adding *s* or *es*.
- If a noun ends in a consonant and *y*, change the *y* to *i* and add *es*.
- Some nouns have a special spelling in the plural form.
- Some nouns have the same spelling for both the singular and plural forms.

Write each noun. If the noun is plural, write its singular form. If the noun is singular, write its plural form.

1. game
2. berries
3. beach
4. city

5. glass
6. deer
7. fly
8. shells

Write each sentence, replacing the underlined word or words with the plural form of the noun.

9. Ringo lay by the man's <u>foot</u> and watched.

10. Was the cat too lazy to chase the <u>mouse</u>?

11. Thomas saw <u>a leaf</u> fall from the tree.

12. Aunt Linzy thought baseball was a good game for <u>a child</u>.

SINGULAR AND PLURAL NOUNS

Rewrite Carlos's letter to his parents. Change the singular nouns to plural nouns.

Dear Mom and Dad,

I am having so much fun at camp! I have never seen so many unusual **(1)** animal before. The **(2)** bird will eat from your hand, and the **(3)** moose will let you pet them. Some of the animals hide in the **(4)** leaf of the **(5)** tree, but I still saw a mother deer with her **(6)** baby. Will you send me some **(7)** box of film? I have so many **(8)** picture I want to take!

Love,

Carlos

9.–10. Choose four nouns from the letter above. Write two sentences of your own, using two of the words in each sentence. You may use singular or plural forms.

CUMULATIVE REVIEW

Write whether each sentence is *declarative, interrogative, imperative,* or *exclamatory.*

1. **Think about Aunt Linzy.**

2. **Linzy is lonely, and she needs us.**

3. **What a cheerful, helpful person she is!**

4. **Could you try to get along with her?**

Write the sentences, capitalizing each proper noun.

5. **That august, the cubs came to wrigley field.**

6. **Thomas's aunt listened as she stroked ringo.**

7. **Thomas talked to donny about aunt linzy.**

8. **Later, thomas and his grandfather played scrabble together.**

Write each noun. If the noun is plural, write its singular form. If the noun is singular, write its plural form.

9. **boy**

10. **feet**

11. **box**

12. **shelf**

13. **child**

14. **puppy**

15. **moose**

16. **book**

POSSESSIVE NOUNS

Rewrite each phrase, using a possessive noun.

1. **the train trip of Chester**
2. **the nest belonging to Tucker**
3. **the conversations of the family**
4. **the snack belonging to the friends**
5. **the whispers among the animals**
6. **the newspaper belonging to the teacher**

Write each sentence, using the possessive form of the noun in parentheses ( ). Then write the plural possessive form of that noun.

7. **Tucker did not expect the (visitor) arrival.**
8. **Could the (insect) story be true?**
9. **With a (child) excitement, Tucker showed Times Square to Chester.**

POSSESSIVE NOUNS

Chester kept a diary about his adventure. Write the following diary entry, replacing the underlined phrases with possessive nouns.

Dear Diary,

When I met **(1)** the friend of Tucker, I was surprised. Harry is a cat! I thought that a cat would be the **(2)** enemy of a mouse. Tucker said that I would like being **(3)** a friend of Harry.

Tonight, I was **(4)** the guest of my friends. We saw some of **(5)** the wonders of this city. We went to Times Square. There I heard **(6)** the roar of the crowd. I saw **(7)** the flashing neon signs of the shops. I thought about **(8)** the home belonging to my family back in the meadow. How different the city seems!

4.

CUMULATIVE REVIEW

Write the plural, singular possessive, and plural possessive form of each singular noun.

1. animal
2. family
3. mouse
4. class
5. woman
6. shop

Write each sentence, using the possessive form of the noun in parentheses ( ). Then circle the simple subject in each sentence you write.

7. Music from (Chester) wings filled the newsstand.
8. The cat purred with pleasure at the (visitor) skill.
9. The tiny (musician) melody was beautiful.
10. Chester played to his (friends) delight.
11. The three friends went to see the (city) sights.
12. Harry admired the (cricket) talent.

ABBREVIATIONS

Write the abbreviation for any word that is spelled out. Write the complete word for any abbreviation.

1. **Mistress**
2. **inches**
3. **Oct.**
4. **Thursday**

5. **Saturday**
6. **Ave.**
7. **Mister**
8. **centimeters**

Write the correct abbreviation for each item.

9. **Jacob Roberts, Junior**
10. **12 ounces**
11. **Doctor Amanda Cortin**
12. **Friday, August 31**

Rewrite these names and addresses, using abbreviations for titles and streets.

13. **Mister Lester Allen**
14. **15 Pleasant Boulevard**
15. **Doctor Terry Corey**
16. **75 Cobb Street**

PRONOUNS AND ANTECEDENTS

Write the pronoun or pronouns in each sentence. If the pronoun has an antecedent, write the antecedent also.

1. Yolanda, I want to tell you about the saguaro cactus.
2. A saguaro is special because it can live for 200 years.
3. After birds move into a saguaro, they call it home.
4. When I told Sarah about the birds, she was surprised about them.
5. If Juan comes over later, I will show him the cactus.

Write each sentence, replacing the underlined words with a pronoun.

6. Sometimes <u>a seed</u> travels with an animal.
7. The desert is a harsh place for <u>young saguaros</u>.
8. <u>Darryl and Michelle</u> take pictures of saguaros.
9. This old saguaro gives <u>a mother woodpecker</u> a nesting place.

PRONOUNS AND ANTECEDENTS

Write each sentence, using the correct pronoun in parentheses ( ). Then write its antecedent.

1. **A saguaro can live 200 years, and (it, they) can grow 50 feet tall.**

2. **Every year, flowers appear, but (it, they) bloom for only one day.**

3. **Although javelinas prefer to eat roots, (he, they) sometimes prey on small animals.**

Write the following paragraph, replacing each underlined word or group of words with a pronoun.

Linda, did **(4)** Linda ever see the desert? My older brother Stephen saw **(5)** the desert last summer when **(6)** Stephen took a train trip to Arizona. Uncle Thomas and Aunt Marie met **(7)** Stephen at the station. **(8)** Uncle Thomas and Aunt Marie drove **(9)** Stephen to their house at the edge of town. Aunt Marie showed Stephen her desert paintings. **(10)** Stephen was fascinated by **(11)** the paintings and couldn't wait to see a saguaro cactus up close.

CUMULATIVE REVIEW

Read the passage and choose the word that belongs in each numbered space.

Marcus hurried to Maya Turner and said, "(1) Turner, look at those saguaros. (2) are magnificent plants."

"Yes," she replied. "(3) should stop for some pictures. Back on Morse (4), we will want souvenirs."

Maya reached for the camera, and Marcus handed (5) a roll of film. "Thank you, Marcus," (6) said.

1. Mrss.
   Mrs
   Mrs.
   mrs.

2. You
   They
   Them
   It

3. They
   He
   Us
   We

4. Boulev.
   Blvd.
   Bvrd.
   bvrd.

5. her
   it
   he
   she

6. you
   they
   she
   it

SUBJECT AND OBJECT PRONOUNS

- A **subject pronoun** takes the place of one or more nouns in the subject of a sentence. The words *I, you, he, she, it, we,* and *they* are subject pronouns. Always capitalize the pronoun *I*.

- An **object pronoun** follows an action verb, such as *see* or *tell,* or a preposition, such as *at, for, to,* or *with.* The object pronouns are *me, you, him, her, it, us,* and *them.*

Write each sentence, replacing the underlined words with a pronoun. Write *subject* or *object* to identify the pronoun.

1. **An invention begins with an idea.**

2. **Some inventions save people time and money.**

3. **The carpet sweeper was invented by Anna and Melville Bissell.**

4. **Later, Melville Bissell improved the design.**

5. **Vacuum cleaners used to be only for rich people.**

6. **Two of the servants were needed to operate one.**

7. **James Murray Spangler invented a lightweight vacuum cleaner.**

8. **Didn't William Hoover buy the rights to that invention?**

SUBJECT AND OBJECT PRONOUNS

Reeba Daniel has started a letter to the Acme Manufacturing Company. Help her finish the letter by choosing the correct pronouns from the box below. You will not use them all.

I	me	we	us	you	he	she	it	they	them

Dear Sir or Madam:

People spend a lot of time doing laundry, and (1) ____ could use some help. (2) ____ have invented a very useful washer/dryer machine. I haven't been able to build a working model of (3) ____ to see if it will really work.

Would (4) ____ like to build a working model for (5) ____? I would be willing to share some of the profits. This invention might make money for both of (6) ____ .

Sincerely,

Reeba Daniel

7.–8. Choose two pronouns from the box that you didn't use in the letter. Write a sentence of your own for each one.

CUMULATIVE REVIEW

Write the pronoun from each sentence. Next to each, write *S* for a subject pronoun and *O* for an object pronoun. Then write the antecedent.

1. **Reeba asked Josh to go biking with her.**
2. **Josh told Reeba that he would like to go.**
3. **After Reeba and Josh rode for two hours, they were tired.**
4. **When Josh and Reeba went to Larry's house, Larry invited them in.**
5. **Larry offered Reeba a cool drink, and Reeba gladly accepted it.**

Write each sentence, replacing the word(s) in parentheses ( ) with a pronoun. Replace the underlined words with a proper noun.

6. **The principal spoke to (the young inventors).**
7. **For two seasons (the girl) played for the team.**
8. **(The parents) are taking their son to (the science fair).**
9. **Will the friends visit (the company) on a day?**
10. **(The mother) and (the children) shopped at the mall all afternoon.**

POSSESSIVE PRONOUNS

- A **possessive pronoun** shows ownership and takes the place of a possessive noun.

- These possessive pronouns are used before a noun: *my, your, her, our,* and *their.*

- These possessive pronouns are not used before a noun: *mine, yours, hers, ours,* and *theirs.*

- *His* and *its* may be used before a noun or not.

Write the possessive pronoun in each sentence. (Hint: Some sentences contain pronouns that are not possessive.)

1. The artist was proud of her work.

2. The people liked their new paintings.

3. "Ours are perfect!" they cried.

4. "I'd like you to meet my friend," said the woman to the artist.

5. "He wants his portrait done, too."

Rewrite each sentence, using the possessive pronoun that is not used right before a noun. Change other parts of the sentence if necessary.

6. Is that your bike?

7. Her bike is the bright-yellow one.

8. The grand prize belongs to them.

POSSESSIVE PRONOUNS

Write the story, replacing the underlined word or words with possessive pronouns.

Pablo burst into Encyclopedia Brown's detective agency and asked for (1) <u>Encyclopedia Brown's</u> help.

"Somebody stole (2) <u>Pablo's</u> nose!" Pablo cried.

(3) <u>The friends'</u> problem had to be solved quickly. Pablo wanted to enter the mayor's contest. But now Pablo couldn't find (4) <u>Pablo's</u> entry! Desmoana said (5) <u>Desmoana's</u> bicycle had nothing to do with the nose's disappearance.

Write each sentence, correcting any errors in the use of possessive nouns.

6. Desmoana said the bike was her.

7. That was mine nose!

8. Ours park doesn't have any statues.

CUMULATIVE REVIEW

Write each sentence, choosing the correct word in parentheses
( ). Write *subject* or *object* to identify each pronoun you choose.

1. After Sally put on the shoes, (she, her) walked to the store.

2. Pablo was waiting for (she, her) there.

3. Manuel said, "Don't wait for (I, me)."

4. As (they, them) played video games, Pablo and Sally talked about school.

5. Rick waved to (they, them) from outside.

6. "Why don't (we, us) go see (he, him), Sally?"

Write each possessive noun, placing *S* next to it if it is singular
and *P* next to it if it is plural. Then write the possessive pronoun
that could replace the underlined words.

7. That <u>man's</u> job is to plan the meeting.

8. The <u>children's</u> toys were left in the rain.

9. <u>Marla's</u> skates got rusty.

10. Those skates had been <u>Mrs. Hom's</u>.

ADJECTIVES AND ARTICLES

- An **adjective** describes a noun or a pronoun. Adjectives can tell *what kind, how many,* or *which one.*

- An adjective can come before the noun it describes, or it can follow a verb such as *is, seems,* or *appears.*

- The adjectives *a, an,* and *the* are called **articles.** Use *a* before a word that begins with a consonant sound. Use *an* before a word that begins with a vowel sound.

Read each sentence carefully. Write the adjectives, including the articles. Then write the noun each adjective describes.

1. **A poor, old woman lived in a tiny house.**

2. **The meals she cooked were simple.**

3. **This thrifty woman kept a vegetable garden.**

4. **She saved for a large, delicious ham.**

5. **She stored it in a cool, dark closet.**

6. **Two tired, hungry men visited one day.**

7. **Did those young travelers enjoy the good supper?**

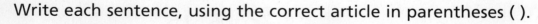

Write each sentence, using the correct article in parentheses ( ).

8. **(An, The) woman served (a, an) hot meal.**

9. **He was not (a, an) honest man.**

10. **(A, An) old woman swept (the, an) sidewalk.**

ADJECTIVES AND ARTICLES

Imagine that the two visitors learned a lesson from their visit with Abuelita. Rewrite their thank-you note to her, adding an adjective or adjectives to describe each underlined noun. Change *a* to *an* if necessary.

Dear Abuelita,

Thank you for opening your (1) <u>home</u> to us. We appreciated the (2) <u>supper</u> of (3) <u>ham</u> and (4) <u>beans</u>. We were glad for a (5) <u>place</u> to sleep.

We are sorry that we seemed ungrateful. You taught us a (6) <u>lesson</u>. It was a (7) <u>surprise</u> to find a (8) <u>brick</u> in place of that (9) <u>ham</u>!

We were lucky to meet a (10) <u>person</u> like you. No matter where our (11) <u>travels</u> take us, we never will forget you!

Sincerely,

The Two Travelers

CUMULATIVE REVIEW

Write each sentence, using the correct possessive pronoun in parentheses ( ).

1. These are (my, mine) opinions.

2. Is that ham (their, theirs)?

3. It was (her, hers) victory.

Write the adjectives in each sentence, including any articles. Then write the noun each adjective describes.

4. The old woman was poor.

5. Each day she ate pinto beans and corn tortillas.

6. A vegetable garden was next to the adobe home.

7. In it she grew speckled beans and red chiles.

8. She sold fresh vegetables on market day.

9. That life seemed simple but happy.

10. One day, she bought a delicious ham.

11. The woman gave each guest a large slice.

12. For the occasion, she served flour tortillas.

13. She set the table with a festive tablecloth.

14. The guests appreciated the special effort.

COMPARING WITH ADJECTIVES

- Add *-er* to most short adjectives to compare two things. Add *-est* to compare one thing with two or more other things.

- Use *more* with longer adjectives to compare two things. Use *most* to compare one thing with two or more other things.

- The adjectives *good* and *bad* have special forms for comparing.

Write each sentence, using the correct comparative form of the underlined adjective.

1. Red's basket was <u>heavy</u> than her friend's basket.

2. That third wolf had the <u>big</u> teeth of all.

3. Miss Muffet was <u>hungry</u> than yesterday.

Write each sentence, using the correct form of the comparing word in parentheses ( ).

4. The smile of the first prince was (more, most) charming than that of the second prince.

5. Was Miss Muffet's visit to the palace the (more, most) exciting experience that she had ever had?

COMPARING WITH ADJECTIVES

Red wrote one more scene for the story. She made a few mistakes with the adjectives, though. Rewrite the lines spoken by the characters, correcting the errors.

1. **MISS MUFFET: This is the most excitingest night of my life!**

2. **FIRST PRINCE: It is the stranger night of my life!**

3. **CINDERELLA: Oh, no! It is getting closerer and closerer to midnight!**

4. **SECOND PRINCE: You seem more worrieder than you did before.**

5. **WOLF: This is the mostest ridiculous outfit I've ever worn.**

6. **RED: You are the worse dancer I've ever seen, Wolf.**

7. **GOLDILOCKS: This is the most latest I've ever been awake.**

8. **BABY BEAR: Me, too! I'm getting exhausteder with each dance.**

Write *simple* or *compound* to identify each sentence. Then write the conjunctions.

1. Red won the prize in the dance contest.
2. Red's dance was creative, and she danced gracefully.
3. The wolf was good, but Red was better.
4. Baby bear depended upon his mother.
5. His mother looked for food, but she couldn't find much.

Write each sentence, using the correct form of the adjective in parentheses ( ).

6. This week's movie was (frightening) than last week's movie.
7. Mel says that it's the (frightening) one he's ever seen.
8. Does this restaurant serve (good) food?
9. Marie believes that it's a (good) restaurant than Fernando's.
10. Paul's idea is a (bad) one.
11. In fact, it's the (bad) idea I've ever heard!

VERBS

- A **verb** is a word that expresses action or being. The main word in the predicate of a sentence is a verb.
- Sometimes the verb in a sentence is a group of two or more words that work together.

Write each sentence. Underline the predicate and circle the verb. Then identify the verb as *action* or *being*.

1. Elephants are the largest land animals.
2. Elephants live in groups, or herds.
3. Their trunks make them different from other animals.
4. The trunk is the elephant's nose.
5. An elephant uses its trunk for many things.

Write the verb group in each sentence.

6. An elephant will carry twigs with its trunk.
7. Elephant tusks are made of ivory.
8. Some tusks can be more than 10 feet long.
9. Elephants will roll in mud.
10. The mud does protect their skin.

VERBS

One of the raja's advisers wrote him a letter. Complete the paragraph, using a verb or verb group from the box below for each blank. You may use some verbs more than once and others not at all.

ordered	want	heard	will listen	will share
collected	hope	are	wonder	think
am	will return	felt	cancel	is

Dear Raja,

   Your people ____ hungry. They ____ when you ____ the rice that you ____ .

   Yesterday, you ____ a feast for your own family and the members of the court. I ____ terrible when I first ____ about this.

   The people ____ you have made a serious mistake. I ____ sure you will agree that this ____ not the right time for such a feast.

   I ____ that you ____ to these words of advice. If you ____ the people to keep loving you, please ____ this feast.

                                    Sincerely,

                                    Your Adviser

CUMULATIVE REVIEW

Read the passage and choose the word or group of words that belongs in each numbered space.

I am one of the (1) in the raja's storehouses. All of our (2) are hungry because of the raja. He is the (3) man I have ever known!

Yesterday, a girl (4) the raja. We were told, "Give the girl one grain of rice. Double that each day until thirty days (5)." These were the (6) instructions we had ever received.

1. workers'
   worker's
   workers
   workeres

2. child
   children
   childs
   childes

3. more selfish
   most selfish
   selfisher
   selfish

4. will visit
   is visiting
   visited
   visit

5. are passing
   passing
   have passed
   is passing

6. strange
   strangerest
   most strangest
   strangest

MAIN AND HELPING VERBS

- A **helping verb** works with the main verb to tell about an action.

- Helping verbs come before main verbs.

- Sometimes another word comes between main and helping verbs.

For each sentence, write the main verb. Then write the helping verb.

1. This fire engine is used for major fires.

2. It could easily hold twenty firefighters.

3. The driver has developed great skill.

4. He will always find the quickest route.

5. The other firefighters do trust his good sense.

Write each sentence, using a helping verb and a form of the verb in parentheses ( ).

6. A gas line (explode).

7. Firefighters (respond) quickly.

8. The trucks (zoom) along.

9. Sirens (wail) loudly.

10. People (jump) out of the way.

MAIN AND HELPING VERBS

Write the paragraph, using the words in the box to complete each sentence. Then underline the helping verbs.

lashed	improving	destroyed	built	lived
expect	try	hang	known	seem

Homes in the 1600s were (1) _____ quickly. Builders had usually (2) _lashed_ together straw bundles for the roofs. If you had (3) _____ back then, you would have (4) _known_ all about firefighting. You could probably (5) _____ a major fire every few weeks.

Early firefighting does (6) _seem_ primitive to modern eyes. Townspeople would (7) _hang_ a bucket near the door. Although the people did (8) _try_ their best, town after town was (9) _Destroyed_. Today, we are constantly (10) _improving_ our firefighting abilities.

11.–12. Write two sentences about school fire drills. In each sentence, use helping verbs and main verbs. Underline the main verbs and circle the helping verbs.

CUMULATIVE REVIEW

Write the main verbs. Then write the helping verbs.

1. Most rural fire companies will use volunteers.
2. Volunteer firefighters certainly do deserve respect.
3. The station house has become a second home for them.
4. Their real jobs will often seem less important.
5. Volunteering could mean a lot to you, too.

Write each sentence, using a helping verb from the box. You may use a helping verb more than once.

are	were	should	was	will
had	do	would	could	

6. The alarm ____ blaring.
7. I ____ hear it from my house.
8. It ____ started at noon.
9. The fire engines ____ respond.
10. They ____ racing down the road.
11. Everyone ____ let them pass.
12. Firefighters ____ save lives.
13. In the old days, fire engines ____ drawn by horses.
14. Sometimes a black-and-white dog ____ run along with the engine.

ACTION AND LINKING VERBS

Write the main verb. Then write *action* or *linking* to tell what kind of verb it is.

1. Many people are in the courthouse.

2. A man in a suit calls the names.

3. Jorge's father feels very happy.

4. The Idris family seems excited.

5. Each new citizen steps to the front.

6. Zeng Yujin opens his package.

7. Small American flags are inside.

8. Two rows of strangers wave flags.

Write each sentence, using the type of verb in parentheses ( ).

9. Kwame (action) the courthouse steps.

10. Efua (linking) Kwame's wife.

11. He (action) snow off his coat.

ACTION AND LINKING VERBS

1.–8. Write the verb in each title. Then tell if it is an *action* or *linking* verb.

"This Land Is Your Land"
"Of Thee I Sing"
"I Am a Yankee Doodle Dandy"
"You Are a Grand Old Flag"
"It Is a Long Way to Tipperary"
"Swing Low, Sweet Chariot"
"Take Me Out to the Ball Game"
"I Left My Heart in San Francisco"

Write one verse of a song of your own. Your song should celebrate being an American. Underline the verbs. Tell whether each verb you use is an action verb or a linking verb.

CUMULATIVE REVIEW

Write the main verbs in each sentence. Then write the helping verbs.

1. Do new citizens vote in elections?
2. They could even serve on a jury.
3. Many new citizens have sponsored relatives.
4. New arrivals should study English and citizenship.
5. Many will become citizens in a few years.
6. Mrs. Trang has just arrived from Laos.
7. Her husband was born in this country.
8. They will enjoy their new life.

Write the verb in each sentence. Then write whether it is *action* or *linking*.

9. One family sits on the courthouse steps.
10. They are thankful for their new lives.
11. They greet each day with excitement.
12. Mr. Trang hopes for a job in Boston.
13. His wife is a very good translator.
14. Their children seem quiet.
15. They speak English well.
16. They go to American schools.
17. They know Vietnamese as well.

PRESENT TENSE

- A verb in the **present tense** shows that the action is happening now or happens over and over.
- A verb should agree with its subject in number.
- Add *s* or *es* to most present-tense verbs when the subject is *he, she, it,* or a singular noun.

Write the present-tense verb in each sentence. Then write whether the verb is *singular* or *plural.*

1. **Everything costs more nowadays.**
2. **People pay ten times as much for sugar.**
3. **They ride in cars to go to the next town.**
4. **A trip by car takes only a few minutes.**

Write each sentence, using the correct present-tense form of the verb in parentheses ( ).

5. **A girl (study) the whole school year.**
6. **Schools often (have) computers.**
7. **Lunchrooms (serve) hot meals.**
8. **Boys and girls (attend) school together.**
9. **A bus (take) them to school.**
10. **A library (provide) books.**

PRESENT TENSE

Write each sentence. Use the pronouns from the box as subjects of the sentences. Use each pronoun only once. Make sure your subjects and verbs agree.

I	You	He	She	It	They

1. ____ see the delivery wagon coming.

2. ____ carries groceries from local farmers.

3. ____ sell their produce to a grocer.

4. ____ hires a driver to deliver it to a housewife.

5. ____ stores the groceries in an icebox.

6. ____ never know how quickly food can go bad!

7.–8. Write pairs of sentences that use singular and plural forms of the present-tense verbs below. Use the pictures to help.

travel

hurry

CUMULATIVE REVIEW

Choose the correct way to write the underlined words.

(1) <u>Many households today has</u> two telephone lines—one for a computer modem and one for regular use. (2) <u>When your using</u> a modem, your telephone (3) <u>line is busy</u>. If (4) <u>you had, only one line,</u> no one can get through.

1. Today many households has

   Many households today are having

   Many households today have

   No mistake

2. When you are using

   When you using

   When you were using

   No mistake

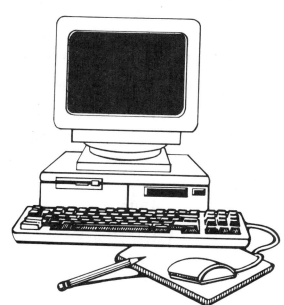

3. lines are busy.

   line has been busy.

   line, is busy.

   No mistake

4. you has only one line,

   you have, only one line

   you have only one line,

   No mistake

PAST AND FUTURE TENSES

- A verb in the **past tense** shows that the action happened in the past. Add *d* or *ed* to regular verbs to form the past tense.

- A verb in the **future tense** shows that the action will happen in the future. Use the helping verb *will* with the main verb to form the future tense.

Write each verb. Then write whether the verb is *past tense* or *future tense*.

1. Janey liked her new teacher very much.
2. She will succeed at the Camp Miller School.
3. Many students will graduate from this school.
4. Janey attended many camp schools over the years.
5. She really dreaded the first day of school.

Write each sentence with the correct form of the verb in parentheses ( ).

6. Miss Peterson (greet—past tense) Janey.
7. Janey (enjoy—future tense) her class.
8. She (skip—past tense) into the room.

PAST AND FUTURE TENSES

1. Write this present-tense paragraph in the past tense.

Janey captures a horned toad. It struggles a bit. Then it rests in her hand. She shows it to her teacher. Miss Peterson chuckles. It is a good thing that Miss Peterson has a sense of humor!

Write the past and future tense for each present-tense verb.

2. **laugh**

3. **believe**

4. **shout**

5. **snore**

6. **scurry**

7. **grin**

8. **reply**

9. **cry**

10. **talk**

11. **study**

CUMULATIVE REVIEW

Read each sentence. Then write the present-tense verbs in the past tense. Write the past-tense verbs in the present tense.

1. Janey studied every day.
2. She places some books on the table.
3. Soon, books surrounded her.
4. Janey opens her reader.
5. She traces some letters on paper.

Write the past and future verb tense for each present-tense verb.

6. complete
7. remark
8. correct
9. erase
10. damage
11. try
12. slip
13. watch
14. carry
15. trap

IRREGULAR VERBS

Skill Reminder

- An **irregular verb** does not end in *ed* in the past tense.
- Some irregular verbs use a different form of the main verb with the helping verb *have, has,* or *had.*

Write a sentence to answer each question. Use the past-tense form of the verb you see in the question.

1. **What time did you go home?**
2. **What did you wear to the party?**
3. **What did you think of the movie?**
4. **When did you begin the book?**
5. **How did you know the answer?**

Write each sentence, using the correct past-tense or helping verb form of the verb in parentheses ( ).

6. **The fiesta had (begin) at dusk.**
7. **First the children (break) the piñata.**
8. **Grandma (bring) out platefuls of food.**
9. **The cousins (throw) confetti all around.**
10. **We all had (wear) our best clothes.**

IRREGULAR VERBS

Write the past-tense form for each present-tense verb.

1. **begin**
2. **break**
3. **bring**
4. **throw**
5. **wear**
6. **know**

Write this present-tense paragraph in the past tense.

 My aunt and uncle are great cooks. They know all the old recipes. They bring out all the ingredients at once. Then Aunt Paz begins the squash filling while Uncle Beto breaks a dozen eggs.

CUMULATIVE REVIEW

Write the verb in each sentence. Then write whether each verb is *past, past with helping verb,* or *future.*

1. We have begun our work.
2. The eggs will look beautiful.
3. I have broken only one.
4. The paints will splatter a bit.
5. I wore my oldest shirt.
6. I used purple and orange.
7. I will use them again.

Write the verbs, changing present-tense verbs to past tense.

8. *Cascarones* are part of my childhood.
9. I begin with a plain egg.
10. I think of a pretty design.
11. Then I decorate the eggshell.
12. Sometimes the shell breaks.
13. Then I throw it away.
14. We fill the eggshells with confetti.
15. I rub confetti in people's hair.
16. My brothers are sneaky.
17. They add flour to the eggshells.
18. That makes quite a mess!

CONTRACTIONS AND NEGATIVES

Write the contraction for each word pair.

1. **it is**
2. **they are**
3. **could not**
4. **has not**

5. **we have**
6. **he had**
7. **are not**
8. **did not**

Write the negative from each sentence.

9. **We never saw such lovely scenery.**

10. **Nowhere on Earth could be so grand.**

11. **Those pioneers have no electricity.**

12. **They could not see very well.**

CONTRACTIONS AND NEGATIVES

1.–5. Write the paragraph, using contractions in place of the underlined words.

Cold weather is not a friend to pioneers. It is a serious enemy. As they are preparing for winter, pioneers do not waste time. They cannot afford to be left without food or heat in the wintertime.

6. Write this paragraph. Correct all double negatives. Use pronouns and contractions correctly.

They aren't never prepared for the cold. Its always a surprise, and their never ready. There isn't nothing warm enough to wear. Even they're boots let in the cold.

CUMULATIVE REVIEW

Write each sentence, using the correct past-tense form of the verb in parentheses ( ).

1. The pioneer (bring) her ax with her.

2. She (wear) a heavy apron.

3. First, she (break) some sticks for kindling.

4. Then, she (throw) them into a basket.

5. The basket (be) full in no time.

Write each sentence. Use a contraction in place of the underlined word or words.

6. <u>Would not</u> you like to own some land?

7. Your window-box garden <u>is not</u> big enough.

8. <u>It is</u> better to have lots of land to till.

9. Imagine that <u>you are</u> living on 50 acres.

10. <u>I am</u> sure that <u>you have</u> thought about it.

11. Personally, <u>I would</u> like to have some horses and sheep.

12. You <u>cannot</u> do that with less than 10 acres.

ADVERBS

- An **adverb** is a word that modifies a verb.
- Adverbs may tell *where, when,* or *how* about a verb.

Write the verb. Then write the adverb that describes each verb.

1. The loggers swung their axes hard.
2. The sound of axes rang out.
3. One hundred trees fell instantly.
4. Finally, the men finished their work.
5. Homeward tramped the tired loggers.

Write whether the underlined adverbs describe *where, when,* or *how.*

6. The massive pines grow <u>upward</u>.
7. <u>Yearly</u>, they produce cones.
8. Squirrels <u>happily</u> collect the cones.
9. They scatter the seeds <u>around</u>.
10. <u>Later</u>, new seedlings sprout.

Write each sentence, adding an adverb that gives the information in parentheses ( ).

11. Paul sawed some tree trunks. (when)
12. He carried fifty logs. (where)

ADVERBS

Write the adverb in each sentence.

1. Sadly, Babe chewed his cud.
2. The ox happily ate pancakes.
3. He awoke early each morning.
4. He politely asked the cook for some chow.
5. For an ox, Babe danced superbly.
6. Daily, he practiced his moves.
7. He dances only for us.
8. Have you seen him yet?
9. Tomorrow, he will dance in a contest.
10. We will clap loudly for Babe.
11. Paul cooks skillfully.
12. He quickly made a huge biscuit for the workers.
13. They smiled happily as he set it on the table.
14. The workers ate the enormous biscuit hungrily.

CUMULATIVE REVIEW

Choose the best way to write each underlined section.

(1) **Paul never saw nothing** like Babe before. (2) **He couldnt imagine** a finer beast. (3) **Babe grew rapid** and soon outweighed his master. Paul (4) **fed him bushels of oats daily**.

1. **Paul never saw nobody**

   Paul ever saw nothing

   Paul never saw anything

   No mistake

2. **He cant imagine**

   He couldn't imagine

   He could n't imagine

   No mistake

3. **Babe grew rapidly**

   Rapid Babe grew

   Babe grew. Rapidly

   No mistake

4. **fed him bushels daily of oats.**

   daily fed him. Oats in bushels.

   in the day fed him bushels of oats.

   No mistake

COMPARING WITH ADVERBS

Write each sentence, using the correct form of the two adverbs in parentheses ( ).

1. The farm stands (farther, farthest) of all from the village.

2. Of all the relatives, TJ's grandparents wept (harder, hardest).

3. TJ recovered (sooner, soonest) than his mother did.

4. The relatives chattered (more rapidly, most rapidly) than birds.

5. They hugged TJ (tighter, tightest) than a warm cocoon.

Write each sentence, using the correct form of the adverb in parentheses ( ). Use more or most where needed.

6. TJ spoke (quietly) than he did at home.

7. His cousins shouted (noisily) of all.

8. Grandfather taught TJ Vietnamese (fast) than his mother could.

9. Of all the relatives, Uncle Thao worked (hard).

COMPARING WITH ADVERBS

Draw the chart. Fill in the holes with the correct form of each adverb.

ADVERBS	COMPARING TWO ACTIONS	COMPARING MORE THAN TWO ACTIONS
1. energetically	more energetically	
2. kindly		most kindly
3. low		
4. sensibly		
5. carelessly		
6. beautifully		
7. well		

Write the sentences, using the adverbs from the chart above.

8. The aunts flapped the sheets ____ of all.

9. Uncle Thao treated his oxen ____ than TJ expected.

10. The cousins behaved ____ of all when they were away from their parents.

11. Mother dressed ____ here than she had back home.

12. In the end TJ adjusted ____ than anybody could have hoped.

CUMULATIVE REVIEW

Write each verb. Then write the adverb that describes the verb. Write whether the adverb describes *where, when,* or *how.*

1. **Uncle Thao hitched the oxen expertly.**
2. **TJ plowed the field crudely.**
3. **The plow often jerked.**
4. **TJ's rows wandered around.**
5. **Then his uncle laughed.**

Draw the chart. Write the correct form of the adverb in the empty boxes.

ADVERBS	COMPARING TWO ACTIONS	COMPARING MORE THAN TWO ACTIONS
6. slowly	more slowly	
7. thoughtfully		
8. high		
9. fortunately		
10. pleasantly		
11. lovingly		
12. late		
13. fast		
14. sweetly		
15. clumsily		

PREPOSITIONS

Make two columns. Label them with the headings **PREPOSITION** and **OBJECT OF THE PREPOSITION**. Read each sentence. Then write the preposition and object of the preposition in the correct columns.

1. I hiked up the steep mountain.

2. Then I wandered through a bog.

3. In the moss I spotted little red plants.

4. Have you ever heard of sundews?

5. To me, they seemed quite pretty.

Use each preposition and object below in a sentence of your own.

PREPOSITION	OBJECT OF THE PREPOSITION
6. across	bridge
7. on	hillside
8. from	them

PREPOSITIONS

Write each preposition and its object.

1. **Rajah pitcher plants grow in Borneo.**

2. **Of all carnivorous plants, they are the largest.**

3. **Their pitchers are the size of footballs.**

4. **The pitcher plant may even dine on small squirrels.**

5. **These plants have been seen by very few people.**

Write the paragraph, using prepositions from the box to complete each sentence. Use each word only once.

under	in	with	up	through	until	off

We went **(6)** ____ Blueberry Hill Road. Then we slipped **(7)** ____ the fence. Butterworts grew **(8)** ____ the field there. I clipped a leaf **(9)** ____ my scissors. A tiny bug fell **(10)** ____ the leaf. **(11)** ____ that moment, I had not realized that these plants were carnivorous. **(12)** ____ careful analysis, I discovered the sticky substance that dissolved the insects.

CUMULATIVE REVIEW

Draw the chart. Fill in the empty boxes with the correct form of each adverb.

ADVERBS	COMPARING TWO ACTIONS	COMPARING MORE THAN TWO ACTIONS
1. quietly	more quietly	
2. thankfully		most thankfully
3. clearly		
4. high		
5. happily		

Make two columns with the headings PREPOSITION and OBJECT OF THE PREPOSITION. Read each sentence. Then write each preposition and object of the preposition in the correct column.

6. Plant the seeds in a flowerpot.

7. Then cover them with green moss.

8. Use rainwater from the water tank.

9. Fertilizer of any kind kills carnivorous plants.

10. Left by themselves, the plants will do well.

PREPOSITIONAL PHRASES

- A **prepositional phrase** includes a preposition, its object, and any words in between.

Write the prepositional phrase in each sentence. Then write the preposition.

1. **Aldo stuck his hand through the bars.**
2. **He petted Lucette with his fingers.**
3. **In a few moments, Lucette was calm.**
4. **After that, she continued eating her corn.**
5. **She picked the kernels off the ear.**
6. **Before long, the ear was picked clean.**

Write each sentence, adding a prepositional phrase.

7. **The parrot's cage sat ____.**
8. **____ , the parrot rested quietly.**
9. **Her corncob lay ____.**
10. **Aldo and Bolivia tiptoed ____.**
11. **____ , Lucette would nap.**
12. **Her dream ____ would delight her.**

PREPOSITIONAL PHRASES

Bolivia wrote about her experience in the rain forest room.
Improve her report by adding prepositional phrases. Use the
phrases in the box or think up your own to replace each
number. Write the revised report.

in the room	**after school**	**of tropical sounds**
out the door	**with birds**	**up a plant**
across the floor	**on my face**	**from the Amazon**
of the snake		

(1) I visited the science room. I brought a parrot (2) named
Lucette. The temperature (3) was quite hot. I soon felt
perspiration (4). A tape (5) played. The room seemed crowded (6).
Monkeys climbed (7). A green snake moved (8). Dr. Osborne was
afraid (9). She soon escaped (10).

CUMULATIVE REVIEW

Make two columns. Label them with the headings PREPOSITION and OBJECT OF THE PREPOSITION. Read each sentence. Then write each preposition and the object of each preposition in the correct column.

1. **Mr. Peters designed a rain forest in a classroom.**
2. **Painted vines hung from the ceiling.**
3. **Pots of tropical plants stood nearby.**
4. **The heater kept the room at a high temperature.**
5. **With a humidifier, Mr. Peters controlled the dampness.**

Write each sentence, adding a prepositional phrase to make it complete.

6. **Mr. Peters's class worked _____.**
7. **_____, the rain forest was completed.**
8. **Students wander _____ every day.**
9. **They like to look _____.**
10. **_____, the plants and animals do well.**

Additional Practice

Grammar

Usage

Mechanics

ADDITIONAL PRACTICE

Sentences

A. Read each group of words, and write whether it is a sentence.

Examples:

People do tricks with yo-yos.
sentence

Are very popular toys.
not a sentence

1. Yo-yos were invented 3,000 years ago in China.

2. Brought to Europe hundreds of years ago.

3. In England, this toy was called a *quiz*.

4. Popular in France, too.

5. In the Philippines, yo-yos were used for a serious purpose.

6. Hunters threw them at animals.

7. An American named Donald Duncan.

8. Duncan visited the Philippines.

9. He was amazed by what people could do with yo-yos.

10. Decided to make toy yo-yos.

B. Identify each sentence. Revise each of the other groups of words to make it a sentence.

Examples:

Lillian Leitzel performed on the flying trapeze. *sentence*

The first person in the Circus Hall of Fame. ***She was the first person in the Circus Hall of Fame.***

11. Lillian was in a circus family.

12. Her mother was a trapeze artist.

13. Her grandmother was one, too.

14. At the age of 84 on the trapeze.

15. As a child, Lillian played the piano well.

16. Dreamed of being a musician.

17. Instead, she joined the family act.

18. She came to this country at the age of 15.

19. She, her mother, and two aunts with the Barnum and Bailey Circus.

20. Lillian Leitzel developed new tricks.

Writing Application Find several incomplete sentences in newspaper or magazine advertisements. Make them into complete sentences.

ADDITIONAL PRACTICE

Declarative and Interrogative Sentences

A. Read each sentence, and write whether it is declarative.

Examples:

Geologists study minerals.
declarative

Why is Monique so serious?
not declarative

1. Monique is hiking across the desert with her grandfather.

2. They are looking for minerals.

3. What is so special about that rock?

4. They will polish it into a smooth stone.

5. Shouldn't Monique choose an easier hobby?

B. Read each sentence, and write whether it is interrogative.

6. Rocks are more than just her hobby.

7. She plans to become a geologist.

8. Where can she learn how to use scientific instruments to help her?

9. Will she attend the Colorado School of Mines?

10. Isn't that college in the town of Golden?

C. Revise the sentences. Make each declarative sentence an interrogative sentence. Make each interrogative sentence a declarative sentence.

Example:

Kyle really did like the neighborhood talent show.

Did Kyle really like the neighborhood talent show?

11. Miss Merlin can do amazing tricks.

12. Were the tickets free?

13. The theater is crowded.

14. The audience was noisy.

15. Are the children getting restless?

16. Miss Merlin finally did appear.

17. Are those flowers on her cape painted in red glitter?

18. Is her act funny?

19. This is Kyle's favorite show.

20. Miss Merlin will pull a fake rabbit from an old hat.

ADDITIONAL PRACTICE

Exclamatory and Imperative Sentences

A. Read each sentence, and write whether it is exclamatory.

Examples:

That cabin must be 100 years old!
exclamatory

Look at this old bottle.
not exclamatory

1. Ask if we can dig for old bottles.

2. She says we're welcome to search!

3. Dig slowly and carefully.

4. My shovel just struck something!

5. I may have found a treasure!

B. Read each sentence, and write whether it is imperative.

6. Put this old flowerpot in the trash.

7. Now you've uncovered something!

8. Bring me the water jug and a rag.

9. What a beautiful bottle this is!

10. Wrap it carefully for the ride home.

C. Read the sentences, and identify each one as an exclamation or a command.

Examples:

I've lost my new sunglasses!
exclamation

Help me look for them.
command

11. Please telephone my friend Jeremy.

12. Ask him to look in his basement.

13. Maybe I left my sunglasses at the park!

14. Ride my bicycle there, Mindy.

15. Dad gave them to me for my birthday!

16. Good sunglasses are expensive!

17. Check on top of Mom's computer.

18. I think I see them on the table!

19. Those are Grandma's!

20. What a disappointment!

21. Answer the telephone.

22. Jeremy has found a pair of sunglasses in his basement!

23. Please answer the door.

24. Mindy found a pair at the park!

25. They can't both be mine!

ADDITIONAL PRACTICE

Simple and Compound Sentences

A. Read each sentence, and write whether it is simple or compound.

Examples:

Kim is running for student council.
simple

The students might elect Lin, or they might vote for one of the others.
compound

1. Candidates will give speeches today.

2. Kim wrote a speech, and she has practiced it.

3. She feels a little nervous.

4. Antonio will speak first.

5. Lin has a plan for the school.

6. Lin's speech is very funny.

7. Kim steps to the front of the room, and she trips over a book on the floor.

8. She opens her mouth, but no words come out.

9. Kim does not expect a victory, but she flashes a victory sign anyway.

10. Antonio wins, and Kim congratulates him.

B. Revise each pair of simple sentences to make a compound sentence.

Example:

Dwight David Eisenhower was elected President in 1952. He was elected to a second term in 1956.

Dwight David Eisenhower was elected President in 1952, and he was elected to a second term in 1956.

11. Eisenhower was born in Texas. He soon moved to Kansas.

12. He was a good student. He was a fine football player in high school.

13. Dwight wanted a college education. His family had very little money.

14. He had one hope for a free education. That was the military.

15. The United States Military Academy chooses a few good students each year. It chose Dwight.

16. Dwight entered the academy. He got a fine education in exchange for service.

17. General Eisenhower led the army to victory during World War II. Seven years later he was elected President.

ADDITIONAL PRACTICE

Subjects and Predicates

A. Write the subject of each sentence.

Example:

Many dogs compete in contests.
Many dogs

1. Kenji throws the Frisbee high.

2. A small dog runs along under it.

3. The dog leaps high into the air.

4. He grabs the Frisbee with his teeth!

5. This talented dog is named Bo.

B. Write the predicate of each sentence.

Example:

Small dogs are often good jumpers.
are often good jumpers

6. Bo is competing for a prize.

7. The crowd cheers loudly for Bo.

8. Kenji cheers, too.

9. Bo's final catch is the best one.

10. He wins the championship!

C. Write the subject and the predicate in each sentence.

Example:

Harvey Ladew led an exciting life.
subject—Harvey Ladew
predicate—led an exciting life

11. New York State was his birthplace.

12. Harvey crossed Africa's desert in his youth.

13. He visited Paris, London, and other famous cities.

14. The traveler settled near Baltimore.

15. Mr. Ladew was a talented gardener.

16. His special skill turned plants into animals.

17. He trimmed bushes into the shapes of horses.

18. A long hedge became waves with swans.

19. A leafy rooster perched on a tree.

20. This skillful gardener created imaginary animals, too.

21. He turned a tree into a unicorn.

22. Ladew tended his garden for fifty years.

ADDITIONAL PRACTICE

Complete and Simple Subjects

A. Read each sentence, and write the complete subject.

Example:

My little brother loses things.
My little brother

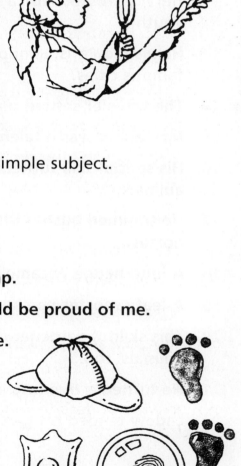

1. A big sister is a good detective.

2. This great detective knows all.

3. My best friend can find clues.

4. Our mother is getting impatient.

5. The swamp is the place to look.

B. Read each sentence, and write the simple subject.

Example:

The best clues are found here.
clues

6. The other kids were in the swamp.

7. The most brilliant detective would be proud of me.

8. I can show you the missing stone.

9. Your solution is not correct.

10. The stone is in my pocket!

C. Write the complete subject in each sentence. Underline the simple subject.

Example:

The rushing river calls to Grandpa and me.
The rushing <u>river</u>

11. The shallow water is still and quiet.

12. My daring grandpa helps me put on my life jacket.

13. My favorite place is the front of the boat.

14. The other seat is for Grandpa.

15. That position is for steering.

16. Our steady course leads between rocks.

17. Two big fish jump in the river.

18. A good meal is important on a long ride.

19. The cool water splashes onto my lap.

20. My delicious sandwich is soaked.

21. A real adventurer doesn't mind.

22. My favorite person is my sporty grandpa.

Writing Application Choose an outdoor activity that you enjoy. Write three sentences that describe when, where, and how you do that activity. Underline your complete subjects, and circle your simple subjects.

ADDITIONAL PRACTICE
Compound Subjects

A. Write the compound subject in each sentence.

Example:

Your school and your community need your help!
Your school and your community

1. **Parents and teachers often help.**

2. **Girls and boys can help, too.**

3. **Clubs and organizations need good officers.**

4. **Good presidents and vice presidents take charge.**

5. **A loud person or a popular student is not always the best leader.**

6. **Friendly classmates and helpful students get lots of votes.**

7. **Honesty and a polite manner count.**

8. **A friend or a family member can help with your campaign.**

9. **Your teachers and classmates will be glad you were elected.**

10. **Hard work and a good attitude pay off in an election.**

B. Write each compound subject. Underline the word that joins the parts of the compound subject.

Example:

A carnival and a circus are planned.
A carnival <u>and</u> a circus

11. Parents and children like circuses.

12. The gym or the field is the place to hold one.

13. Our teacher and the principal will take part.

14. Clowns and other performers will entertain our guests.

15. Both happy clowns and sad clowns are fun to watch.

16. Smiles or frowns are painted on their faces.

17. Makeup and silly clothes are all we need.

18. Lions and tigers are hard to get.

19. Mr. Dowling and his helpers will bring some ponies.

20. Balloons and streamers make the circus fun.

ADDITIONAL PRACTICE

Complete and Simple Predicates

A. Write each complete predicate.

Example:

Barney cheers up many patients.
cheers up many patients

1. **This dog visits Valley Hospital.**

2. **He greets his friends with barks.**

3. **Mr. Fletcher shakes hands.**

4. **Jimmy teaches Barney tricks.**

5. **Evelyn feeds Barney pieces of bacon.**

B. Write each simple predicate.

Example:

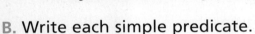

Phil scratches Barney's head.
scratches

6. **A woman takes Barney for a walk.**

7. **Mr. Fong had an operation.**

8. **He missed Barney's visits.**

9. **This friendly man calls for Barney.**

10. **Barney licks his hand happily.**

C. Read the sentences. Write the complete predicate in each sentence. Underline the simple predicate.

Example:

The cargo ship struck a huge rock far out in the Pacific Ocean.

<u>struck</u> *a huge rock far out in the Pacific Ocean*

11. The rock damaged the ship.

12. The crew grabbed life jackets.

13. They boarded the lifeboat quickly.

14. The crew members lowered it into the sea.

15. The captain started the engine.

16. The crew shook their heads sadly.

17. The cargo ship was beyond repair.

18. The lifeboat served them well, though.

19. People on shore sent rescue planes.

20. Several planes searched for the crew.

21. One had a pigeon aboard.

22. The bird spotted orange life jackets.

23. The plane took the crew to land.

ADDITIONAL PRACTICE
Compound Predicates

A. Write each compound predicate.

Example:

Dolphins leap and splash in the sea.
leap and splash in the sea

1. These mammals act playful and are intelligent.

2. They solve problems and communicate.

3. Dolphins find people and save their lives.

4. One legend is old and seems odd.

5. A sailor fell overboard and nearly drowned.

6. A dolphin circled around him and then swam up to him.

7. The sailor grabbed the dolphin and held on.

8. The dolphin brought him close to land and then pushed him toward shore.

9. The sailor swam to shore and told of his amazing rescue.

10. Other legends describe similar rescues and fascinate listeners.

B. Read the sentences. Write each compound predicate. Underline the word that joins the parts of the compound predicate.

Example:

Bloodhounds search for missing people and often find them.

search for missing people <u>and</u> often find them

11. A hiker loses sight of his group and tries to find his way back.

12. His friends call him and look all around.

13. The sheriff calls the search leader and then drives to the forest.

14. The search leader arrives and opens the back of her station wagon.

15. The sheriff asks for the hiker's jacket and holds it toward two dogs.

16. The hounds sniff the jacket and run quickly into the woods.

17. The dogs bark and whine as a signal.

18. The hiker laughs and pats the dogs.

19. Each hero gets a dog biscuit or receives another treat.

ADDITIONAL PRACTICE
Nouns

A. Read each sentence and write the nouns.

Example:

The Arabic language gave us the name of that tall animal.

language, name, animal

1. The tallest mammal in the world is the giraffe.

2. Giraffes have long legs and necks.

3. These animals live on the plains.

4. These graceful creatures eat plants.

5. Giraffes eat leaves from the tops of trees.

6. This food is too high for other animals to reach.

7. Herds travel across the land.

8. Many animals visit wells in the morning and the evening.

9. This special group seldom drinks from streams or lakes.

10. Their water comes from the things they eat.

B. List each noun in the sentences below.

Example:

Scientists can tell the favorite food of a bird from the shape of its beak.
Scientists, food, bird, shape, beak

11. Hummingbirds sip nectar from plants.

12. These birds also eat insects and spiders.

13. The bugs are good sources of protein.

14. Toucans have large beaks.

15. Their bills reach fruit in prickly bushes.

16. Macaws have powerful jaws.

17. These parrots crack nuts with hard shells.

18. Visitors must keep their fingers away from the cage with this animal in it.

19. Hawks, falcons, and eagles catch prey in the daytime.

20. These divers can soar through the air.

ADDITIONAL PRACTICE
Common and Proper Nouns

A. Write the common nouns in each sentence.

Example:

Many coyotes roam the open prairies.
coyotes, prairies

1. Coyotes can live through the long, cold winters in the Rocky Mountains.

2. These animals often hunt in teams.

3. Even the pups have sharp eyes.

4. Adults may surround a large animal.

5. These hunters also eat fruit.

B. Write the proper noun in each sentence.

Example:

Coyotes live in the United States.
United States

6. Do they sing to the moon in Utah?

7. They do in California.

8. In Canada, coyotes stalk sheep.

9. The coat of the coyote protects it from harsh weather in Maine.

10. These animals like the heat of the Southwest.

C. Read the sentences. List all the nouns. Underline any proper nouns.

Example:

Snakes are found on every continent except Antarctica.

snakes, continent, <u>Antarctica</u>

11. The cobra lives in many parts of Asia.

12. Most mongooses live on that continent, too.

13. Rudyard Kipling wrote a story about these two animals.

14. Chameleons live in Europe, Africa, and Asia.

15. These lizards can change the color of their skin.

16. Scientists have discovered these reptiles do not change to blend into their surroundings.

17. My teacher says their color changes with their moods.

18. Many camels live in the Middle East.

19. The animals in the Sanford Zoo have their own areas.

ADDITIONAL PRACTICE

More Proper Nouns

A. Read the sentences and write each proper noun.

Example:

Explorers left Russia in 1741.
Russia

1. The leader was Vitus Bering, who was from Denmark.

2. Georg Wilhelm Steller, a scientist from Germany, was part of the expedition.

3. The explorers set sail across an icy sea on a Tuesday.

4. Near the Commander Islands, the scientist saw a creature that looked like a giant seal.

5. This sea cow was later named after Steller.

6. Later, on the way back to Siberia, fog forced the ship to land on an island.

7. By May, the crew members were starving.

8. In June of 1742, the survivors found food.

9. The Bering Sea was named in honor of the commander.

B. Proofread the sentences. Write them so that all proper nouns are capitalized.

Example:

I read a book on pandas last saturday.
I read a book on pandas last Saturday.

10. **Now I want to go to the zoo on labor day.**

11. **Giant pandas once lived in many parts of china and tibet.**

12. **Now they live only in sichuan, in china.**

13. **About a hundred pandas live in the wolong nature reserve there.**

14. **Scientists in asia and north america worry that pandas may become extinct.**

15. **The ministry of forestry is working to save this animal.**

16. **The world wildlife fund helps, too.**

Writing Application Do some research about a state you would like to visit. Write a paragraph describing some of the things you would do and places you would see. Underline the proper nouns.

ADDITIONAL PRACTICE

Singular and Plural Nouns

A. Write the singular nouns in each sentence.

Example:

Many unusual creatures live on the continent of Australia.
continent, Australia

1. The emu is a large flightless bird.

2. The platypus has fur but lays eggs.

3. The echidna looks like a porcupine but eats ants.

4. The kangaroo is a marsupial.

5. A mother carries her helpless baby in her pouch.

B. Write the plural noun or nouns in each sentence.

Example:

Kangaroos live in dry lands.
Kangaroos, lands

6. Kangaroos hop on their hind legs.

7. Wallabies and koalas are marsupials.

8. Penguins live on the coast.

9. There are hundreds of lizards.

10. Geckos can walk on ceilings.

C. Write each underlined singular noun. Then write its plural form.

Example:

A wild <u>animal</u> lives in Alaska.
animal, animals

11. A <u>wolf</u> howls at the moon.
12. A <u>rabbit</u> runs across a field.
13. A <u>fox</u> is chasing it.
14. A <u>moose</u> shakes its antlers.
15. A bear cub swats at a <u>butterfly</u>.
16. An <u>airplane</u> soars through the sky.
17. It startles a <u>deer</u>.
18. A grizzly bear catches a <u>fish</u>.
19. A <u>mouse</u> makes a <u>home</u> in the wall of a cabin.
20. An <u>eagle</u> dives toward a tree.
21. A <u>squirrel</u> scurries inside a hole.

ADDITIONAL PRACTICE
Possessive Nouns

A. Read each sentence and write the possessive noun.

Example:

A chipmunk took a raisin from my sister's plate.
sister's

1. Some of Colorado's wild animals are not afraid of people.

2. A porcupine chewed my aunt's hat.

3. The blue jays' manners are not very good.

4. One ate part of Grandma's sandwich.

5. Deer eat from our family's garden.

6. My bean plants were a doe's dinner.

7. My father's dream is to have squirrels that don't make any noise.

8. The squirrels' favorite tree is the one beside my bedroom window.

9. I am going to borrow my aunt's camera.

10. I can become America's greatest wildlife photographer.

Writing Application Imagine that you are an animal keeper at a zoo. Write down some ideas for animal care. Use possessive nouns in your writing.

B. Revise each sentence by replacing the underlined group of words with a word group containing a possessive noun.

Example:

<u>The cat of my friend</u> seems unusually smug.
My friend's cat

11. <u>The history of that animal</u> is enough to make it proud.

12. <u>People of Egypt</u> tamed wild African cats 2,000 years ago.

13. Before then, cats did not have <u>the role of a pet</u>.

14. <u>The work of the cats</u> was valuable.

15. <u>The problems of the Egyptians</u> with hunger and disease were solved.

16. The cats kept <u>the germs of the rats</u> from spreading.

17. <u>The hunting skill of a feline</u> is good.

18. <u>The appreciation of the pharaohs</u> was great.

ADDITIONAL PRACTICE

Singular and Plural Possessive Nouns

A. Write the singular possessive nouns.

Example:

A dog is a human's best friend.
human's

1. A poodle's curly hair makes it cute.

2. My cousin's spaniel is very loyal.

3. Collies are a herder's dream.

4. A shepherd's work is never done.

5. A watchdog's protection helps many.

B. Write the plural possessive nouns.

Example:

People have relied on dogs' talents for at least 12,000 years.
dogs'

6. Many breeds' skills are useful.

7. The hounds' short legs help them.

8. This breed can follow small animals' movements through heavy brush.

9. Huge Saint Bernards have been responsible for some people's rescues.

10. Bloodhounds' keen noses help them hunt for lost hikers.

C. Revise each sentence. Make the underlined words a possessive noun, and then underline it.

Example:

Do you like the bright colors <u>of the toucans</u>?
Do you like the <u>toucans'</u> bright colors?

11. We're learning about the amazing animal life <u>of Costa Rica</u>.

12. The diet <u>of a toucan</u> is fruits, nuts, and insects.

13. You may see the long legs <u>of a crane</u> sticking out of the water.

14. Gulls and pelicans nest on the rocks <u>of the shore</u>.

15. The flights <u>of a bat</u> begin at dusk.

16. Fruit bats and vampire bats live in the forests <u>of the area</u>.

17. The homes <u>of sloths</u> are in the treetops.

18. The slow speed <u>of a sloth</u> makes it easy to spot.

19. The cats <u>of the jungle</u> are jaguars and ocelots.

ADDITIONAL PRACTICE
Pronouns

A. Read each sentence, and write the pronoun or pronouns.

Example:

Robin and Paul's garden has many weeds in it.
it

1. The two of them grow plants.

2. She reads about weeds.

3. He searches through plant catalogs for odd fruits and vegetables.

4. They try to grow them in the garden.

5. "We grow many things," Robin said.

6. "A friend helped us plant popcorn last spring," Paul said.

7. "I will let you try the popcorn later in the afternoon," he said to me.

8. "You should look at the plants," Robin said proudly.

9. "What are they?" I asked.

10. "They are oxeye daisies, the prettiest weeds in the garden!" she said.

B. Revise each sentence. Replace the underlined word or words with a pronoun.

Example:

Jamie Jobb wrote <u>a book titled *My Garden*</u>.
Jamie Jobb wrote it.

11. <u>Jamie Jobb</u> wrote the book for ten-year-olds.

12. "<u>My sons and I</u> enjoy gardening," Jamie said.

13. <u>A garden</u> is a good place to learn.

14. A gardener quickly learns about <u>insects</u>.

15. <u>Birds</u> like gardens with fruit trees.

16. <u>Martha Weston</u> drew all the pictures for Jamie Jobb's book.

17. <u>The yellow flowers</u> are daffodils.

18. We bring <u>daffodils</u> to my grandparents each Sunday during spring.

Writing Application Work with a partner. Each person should write a summary of a story without using any pronouns at all. Trade papers. Replace some of your partner's nouns with pronouns.

ADDITIONAL PRACTICE

Subject and Object Pronouns

A. Write the subject pronouns.

Example:

We eat potatoes grown in Idaho.
We

1. They came from Henry Spalding.

2. He settled in Idaho in 1836.

3. We believe he brought the first potatoes there.

4. It was this man who gave potatoes to Nez Percé families.

5. They had never seen potatoes.

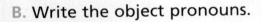

B. Write the object pronouns.

Example:

Families planted them in the spring.
them

6. Bad weather ruined the crops for them.

7. The next year, a visitor to Spalding's mission wrote about him.

8. This time the Nez Percé had good crops that helped them.

9. A traveler was glad they gave food to her.

10. She made it into a meal.

C. Replace each underlined group of words with a pronoun. Write *subject* or *object* after each pronoun you write.

Example:

Bob and I planted sugar maple trees for my aunt and uncle.

We—subject

11. The trees will grow to be 100 feet tall.

12. My uncle will tap the trees.

13. My uncle sometimes collects gallons of sap from each tree.

14. He and my aunt will boil it to make syrup.

15. They are going to share it with Bob and me.

16. My aunt buys these trees at the nursery.

17. I learned from my aunt that maple trees have winged seeds.

18. My aunt can identify all of the thirteen species of maple trees in the United States.

ADDITIONAL PRACTICE
Possessive Pronouns

A. Read the sentences and write each possessive pronoun.

Example:

"My office is near the ocean," Aunt Shirlene explained.
My

1. My aunt is our favorite marine biologist.

2. We visited her apartment last year, and then she came to see ours.

3. "Please show us your slides!" we asked.

4. Aunt Shirlene takes photos of manatees with her underwater camera.

5. "I'm studying their habitats," she said.

6. She told us about their huge appetites.

7. A manatee would eat its weight in plants each day if it could.

8. She asked Dad if she could borrow his slide projector.

9. She showed us a slide of a manatee with a scar across its back.

10. "I hope you're more careful with your motorboat than this driver was," said my aunt.

B. Show how you could revise the sentences. Write a possessive pronoun to replace each underlined word or group of words.

Example:

"Mitch, would you lend me <u>Mitch's</u> watch?" Zoila asked.

your

11. "Oh, that's right. <u>Zoila's</u> watch is broken," Mitch replied.

12. "Did Burt lend you <u>Burt's</u> map?" I asked.

13. "No, Bud and Kay lent me <u>Bud and Kay's</u>," she said.

14. She was ready for <u>Zoila's</u> hike.

15. "Where did I put <u>Zoila's</u> camera?" Zoila exclaimed.

16. "You put it in <u>Zoila's</u> backpack," Mitch said to Zoila.

17. She shook <u>Mitch's and my</u> hands.

18. "Thanks for <u>Mitch's</u> watch," she told Mitch.

19. "How is <u>the camera's</u> battery?" I asked.

Writing Application The chart below shows what three people brought on a hike. Use the chart to write three sentences using possessive pronouns.

Juan	water bottles
Simon	snacks
Brendan	first-aid kit

ADDITIONAL PRACTICE
Adjectives and Articles

A. Write the adjectives in these sentences. (Do not write the articles.)

Example:

Their red tomatoes are big!
red, big

1. Martin collects old postcards of giant vegetables.

2. The carrots are long and fat.

3. If someone cut into one onion, a thousand people would cry huge tears!

4. You could make jam for an army from a gigantic strawberry!

5. Paul Bunyan might slip on the peel of a monstrous banana!

B. Write the articles in these sentences.

6. A farmer unloads a huge orange pumpkin.

7. One gourd weighs an amazing amount!

8. A woman from Gresham, Oregon, thrills the crowd with her golden giant.

9. The winner weighs 706 pounds!

10. The pumpkin contest is a success.

C. Revise the sentences. Replace each underlined word with an adjective that is more descriptive. You may need to change the article, too.

Example:

The people at the state fair are a <u>special</u> group. *The people at the state fair are an extraordinary group.*

11. The vegetables there were <u>big</u>.

12. The winning pie was <u>good</u>.

13. My ride on the Wheel of Fear was <u>fun</u>.

14. Native Americans performed an <u>old</u> dance.

15. A <u>neat</u> woman taught me about quilts.

16. A band played <u>nice</u> music in a tent.

17. A storyteller told an <u>interesting</u> story.

18. A <u>loud</u> pig escaped from the livestock area.

19. It led dozens of people on a <u>big</u> chase.

20. Finally, its <u>tired</u> owner caught it.

ADDITIONAL PRACTICE

Adjectives That Compare: *-er, -est*

A. Read each sentence and write the adjective that compares.

Example:

Bill's plant has the longest vines I've ever seen!
longest

1. His family had the prettier of the two yards.

2. Now the world's largest vine has taken over.

3. Margie Susuki's nicest ball got lost.

4. Bill and Margie searched in their oldest clothes.

5. The yard is denser than a jungle!

6. Margie got tangled in the longest vines.

7. When she tried to move, they got even tighter.

8. Bill went to the largest hardware store in town.

9. He bought the sharpest clippers.

10. The yard is much cleaner without that odd plant!

B. Revise each sentence. Change the underlined adjective so that it compares two things or more than two things. You may need to change or add other words, too.

Example:

Those pumpkins are <u>big</u>.
Those pumpkins are bigger than mine.

11. Ralph bought his seeds at a <u>large</u> garage sale.

12. The package had <u>odd</u> instructions.

13. His pumpkin plants looked <u>weird</u>.

14. Their leaves were <u>strong</u>.

15. Their habit of swatting flies made Ralph <u>happy</u>.

16. The pumpkins could also make <u>high</u> jumps.

17. The pumpkins' skin had a <u>dull</u> color.

18. The neighborhood children have a <u>neat</u> attraction right in their backyard!

ADDITIONAL PRACTICE

Adjectives That Compare: *more, most*

A. Write each adjective that compares.

Example:

That is the most unusual plant of all.
most unusual

1. It thought socks were the most wonderful thing it had ever tasted.

2. Karen could think of things more delicious than socks.

3. The most helpful plant would eat her brother's tuba.

4. A television-eating plant is more useful.

5. Maybe the plant would swallow her sister's most disgusting perfume.

6. Karen could not think of anything more fun to watch!

7. She found the most beautiful plant book.

8. The information was the most boring she had read, though.

9. The plant itself was more interesting!

10. A biologist would be the most qualified person to ask about it.

B. Revise the sentences to add *more* or *most* to each underlined adjective. You may need to add other words, too.

Example:

Natural wonders are <u>valuable</u>.
Natural wonders are more valuable than all the money in the world.

11. The history of our river is an <u>interesting</u> tale.

12. Long ago, the river was <u>beautiful</u>.

13. The water made the nearby land <u>gorgeous</u>.

14. That area had <u>colorful</u> plant life.

15. Wild animals had <u>outstanding</u> drinking water.

16. Seeing badgers come to the water's edge was <u>exciting</u>.

17. Returning the polluted river to a more natural state was <u>difficult</u>.

18. The restoration has been <u>amazing</u>!

19. The change has helped make the earth an <u>attractive</u> place.

ADDITIONAL PRACTICE

Special Forms for Comparing

A. Read the sentences, and write each form of the words *good* and *bad.*

Example:

Doing something fun can help you feel
better

1. My best friend moved away.

2. Then, last week I caught a bad cold.

3. I felt worse each day.

4. I thought this was going to be the worst summer vacation ever!

5. My friend Geri said that reading a book would help me feel better.

6. She said that *The Incredible Journey* is a good book.

7. It's the best book I've read!

8. Geri and I began making our own wilderness book, and I felt better.

9. Geri is good at writing.

10. I'm a better artist, though.

B. Read each sentence. Write the word in parentheses that best completes each sentence.

Example:

Your celery stalk is the (better, best) of all the food puppets.
best

11. Making talking vegetable puppets was the (worstest, worst) idea I ever had.

12. I was much (worse, worst) than my classmates at making puppets.

13. Then I became (better, gooder) at it.

14. John's carrot looked much (worse, worser) than mine.

15. Suno said her tomato was the (worse, worst) puppet.

16. Her eggplant puppet will look much (better, best).

17. The (best, goodest) puppets are usually not the most realistic.

18. Sasha's new broccoli puppet is (better, best) than his last one because it's brighter.

19. The (bestest, best) part is giving the show.

ADDITIONAL PRACTICE
Verbs

A. Read each sentence, and write the verb.

Example:

Nine planets revolve around our sun.
revolve

1. Pluto is the planet farthest from the sun.

2. It circles the sun every 248 years.

3. Its temperature drops below -350°F.

4. Pluto was unknown to scientists 100 years ago.

5. Percival Lowell estimated the location of the planet in 1915.

6. He never found the planet.

7. In 1930, Clyde Tombaugh studied the sky with a powerful telescope.

8. He took many photographs through the telescope.

9. Three of his photographs showed a distant planet.

10. In 1978, astronomers discovered a satellite of Pluto.

B. Write the complete predicate of each sentence. Underline the verb.

Example:

Astronomers study the planets and the stars.
<u>study</u> the planets and the stars

11. Stephen Hawking is a famous astronomer.

12. He studies mysteries of the universe.

13. Black holes seem strange to many of us.

14. These objects are invisible.

15. The gravity of black holes is very strong.

16. Black holes pull nearby comets and planets inside them.

17. Light from nearby stars disappears into black holes, too.

18. Astronomers found these strange holes for the first time about twenty-five years ago.

Writing Application Use a thesaurus to find synonyms for the verbs in the sentences above. Rewrite the sentences with the new verbs. How has the meaning of each sentence changed? Share your ideas with a partner.

ADDITIONAL PRACTICE

Action Verbs

A. Read each sentence, and write the action verb.

Example:

The alarm rang at 5 A.M.

rang

1. Vanetta jumped out of bed.
2. She dressed herself quickly.
3. Then she helped her mother with breakfast.
4. Vanetta poured the cereal.
5. Vanetta and her mother drove away from their house before dawn.
6. They headed straight for the space shuttle launch site.
7. Vanetta's mother parked in a public viewing area.
8. Vanetta spotted the shuttle's giant fuel tank.
9. The radio announcer reported the launch countdown.
10. The space shuttle *Discovery* rose swiftly.

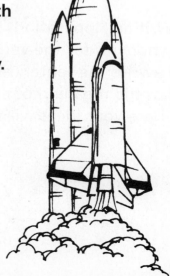

B. Replace the underlined verb in each sentence with a stronger action verb.

Example:

The movie audience <u>looked</u> at the planet's weird landscape.
stared

11. A volcano <u>put</u> fiery rocks into the sky.

12. Captain Wong <u>moved</u> away on her space scooter.

13. Boulders <u>came</u> down all around her.

14. The captain <u>spoke</u> loudly into her wrist telephone.

15. Suddenly, a giant lizard <u>came</u> out from behind a rock!

16. With a snarl, it <u>went</u> toward her.

17. Captain Wong <u>took</u> her camera.

18. Despite the danger, she <u>made</u> several photographs.

19. Then she <u>drove</u> away.

ADDITIONAL PRACTICE
Linking Verbs

A. Read each sentence, and write the linking verb.

Example:

A UFO is an unidentified flying object.
is

1. Today the sky seems unusually dark.

2. The air feels still and heavy.

3. Two space creatures are in our backyard!

4. Each creature is rather short.

5. The creatures' hands and feet are green and rubbery.

6. One's voice seems oddly familiar.

7. I am not afraid of these space aliens.

8. The two creatures are my little brother Max and his friend Dillon.

9. They are in their costumes.

10. Max and Dillon became space aliens for a neighborhood play.

B. Write the verb in each sentence. Then tell whether it is a linking verb or an action verb.

Example:

A balloon is a bag full of air.
is—linking verb

11. Many hot-air balloons are colorful.

12. Our balloon is orange and green.

13. At first my friend and I felt afraid.

14. The pilot spoke kindly to us.

15. She became an expert balloonist several years ago.

16. A gas jet heats the air in the balloon.

17. Now we are high over the valley.

18. The morning air seems very still.

19. The balloon rises toward the clouds.

20. The history of ballooning is interesting.

21. The Montgolfier brothers of France built the first hot-air balloon in 1783.

ADDITIONAL PRACTICE
Main Verbs

A. Read each sentence, and write the main verb.

Example:

Alicia has collected hundreds of coins.
collected

1. Alicia is sorting the coins in her collection.

2. She has received a box of pennies.

3. Alicia's great-grandfather had collected some of the pennies.

4. He had saved a penny from the year 1794.

5. Alicia has added many coins to the collection.

6. She is putting her oldest dime away.

7. She will display it tomorrow at the hobby show.

8. She has won a blue ribbon before.

9. Alicia's principal and teachers are serving as judges.

10. They will see her collection for the first time.

Writing Application Imagine that you are in a contest involving a sport or hobby you enjoy. Write a paragraph about what you are doing, seeing, hearing, and feeling. Underline the main verbs in your paragraph.

B. Write the verb phrase in each sentence. Underline the main verb.

Example:

An old sea chest has disappeared from the Bankston Museum.

has <u>disappeared</u>

11. The police are finding no clues.

12. They have asked a young detective for help.

13. Hector Fernandez is becoming famous.

14. He has solved eight cases already this year.

15. His parents have set one rule for their son.

16. He will do schoolwork before detective work.

17. This Saturday, Hector Fernandez will solve six long-division problems.

18. Then he will visit the Tidy Attic Antique Store.

19. Hector Fernandez will find the answer to another mystery!

ADDITIONAL PRACTICE
Helping Verbs

A. Read each sentence, and write the helping verb.

Example:

Shana is always discovering something brand-new.
is

1. Today she is watching ants.

2. She had stared at something all morning.

3. The ants have carried sand all the way across the ant farm.

4. They will lift loads bigger than themselves.

5. That load will be too heavy for the ant!

6. Shana and I are counting ants quickly.

7. How many were living in one place?

8. Shana's questions are making her curious.

9. We will find some answers.

10. I am looking in the encyclopedia!

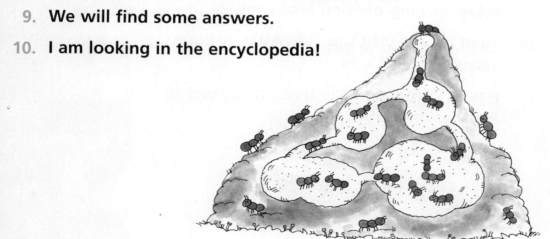

B. Write the verb phrase in each sentence. Underline the helping verb.

Example:

Many famous authors have written mysteries.
<u>*have*</u> *written*

11. Carl is writing a mystery, too.

12. He will plan his story carefully.

13. Someone in his story has hidden a chest.

14. Someone else had looked for clues.

15. Who will be the mystery person?

16. Carl is keeping a plan in mind.

17. He was listing details about the story events.

18. He is using some of these as clues.

19. We will keep other details secret.

20. He has also created an interesting main character.

21. Carl had chosen a young person as his detective.

22. This character will solve the mystery.

ADDITIONAL PRACTICE

Present Tense

A. Read each sentence, and write the present-tense verb or verbs.

Example:

Mrs. Frisby needs help.
needs

1. I like the book *Mrs. Frisby and the Rats of NIMH.*

2. Rats become very intelligent as part of an experiment.

3. Scientists study the rats, and they learn more about the mysteries of intelligence.

4. The rats grow very smart, and they escape from their cages.

5. They run away to the countryside.

6. The rats study agriculture.

7. They want their own farm.

8. Mrs. Frisby, a mouse, needs the rats' help with a problem.

9. The rats have fond memories of her late husband.

10. This book won the John Newbery Medal, and it is my favorite.

B. Write the correct present-tense form of the verb in parentheses ( ).

Example:

Frank (help) vacationers.
helps

11. He (operate) a small fishing boat.

12. The boat (carry) people out onto the lakes.

13. It (travel) through small canals from one lake to the other.

14. The fishing boat (stop) often.

15. People (board) the boat outside Frank's tackle shop.

16. Frank (raise) his own bait.

17. At the sound of a car horn, Frank (look) around.

18. He always (greet) fishers with a smile.

19. He (like) to tell stories about "the one that got away."

20. Then he (help) the guests bait their hooks and cast their lines.

Writing Application What kinds of businesses are part of your community? Choose a business. Write a few sentences about what it makes or does. Use present-tense verbs in your sentences.

ADDITIONAL PRACTICE
Past Tense

A. Write each past-tense verb.

Example:

The mayor handed awards to community helpers.
handed

1. One woman transported elderly people to their doctors' appointments.

2. Another woman cooked for them.

3. An elderly man read books to them.

4. Fourth graders printed letters for people in a nursing home.

5. A young woman conducted a ballet class at a child care center.

6. A woman in a wheelchair guided children on tours of the art museum.

7. A teenager handled errands for people.

8. A husband and wife demonstrated crafts at the county museum.

9. A college student coached the Special Olympics team.

10. The mayor said that community helpers are the true heroes of our time.

B. Revise each sentence. Change the verb from present tense to past tense.

Example:

A boy sails from Norway to America with his family.

A boy sailed from Norway to America with his family.

11. He travels west to California at the age of 24.

12. He discovers only a little gold.

13. He purchases a farm with the gold.

14. He changes his last name from Tostenson to Thompson.

15. In 1856, he answers a newspaper ad.

16. The government needs a mail carrier for the long, cold winter.

17. Snow closes the trails through the high Sierra Nevada mountains in early October.

18. Thompson crosses the mountains on skis.

19. Miners and mountain families depend on "Snowshoe" Thompson.

ADDITIONAL PRACTICE
Irregular Verbs

A. Write the verb in parentheses that best completes each sentence.

Example:

A hiss (come, came) from the darkest corner of the room.

came

1. "This is the most boring game I've ever (saw/seen)," groaned Walker.

2. "I (have/had) a better game, but I lost it," Shawn whined.

3. The baby-sitter (think/thought) this would be the longest evening ever.

4. "What a waste of time," Walker (say/said).

5. When he (took/takes) a turn, he landed on a lion.

6. The lion (ate/eat) the armchair!

7. Can you guess what it (did/do) next?

8. The lion (run/ran) out the door.

9. It (drove/drive) away in a truck.

10. A tiger (rode/ride) with it.

B. Revise each sentence. Change the verb or verbs to past tense.

Example:

Hobie takes his next turn.
Hobie took his next turn.

11. **The box says "An Adventure Game."**

12. **The game has a funny-looking board.**

13. **We see a fierce gorilla on square 16.**

14. **Square 23 has a spooky cave.**

15. **Ki thinks the bird on square 41 looks angry.**

16. **Yori says, "What a strange game!"**

17. **He gives the instructions from the box.**

18. **A shiny spinner comes with the game.**

19. **The rules say "for brave players."**

20. **The game goes quickly.**

21. **Hobie goes to a square with a bug.**

22. **Large red ants eat our lunch.**

23. **Yori says the game is over.**

ADDITIONAL PRACTICE

Future Tense

A. Write the verbs that are in the future tense.

Example:

Tomorrow we will visit one of America's largest cattle ranches.

will visit

1. We will fly over the ocean for hours.

2. Our airplane will land on the slope of a volcano.

3. Then we will ride horses.

4. Instead of beef jerky, we will sample *see moi*, which are salty Chinese plums.

5. The cowhands on the ranch will call themselves *paniolos*.

6. Our tour of Parker Ranch will stretch across many miles of the big island of Hawaii.

7. We will learn about the history of ranching in the Hawaiian Islands.

8. In the afternoon, we will listen to a talk about King Kamehameha the Great.

9. We will see the remains of the king's home at Kailua tomorrow morning.

10. After that we will head home.

B. Revise each sentence. Change the verb to the future tense.

Example:

The temperature falls rapidly.
The temperature will fall rapidly.

11. A blanket of cold air settles on the valley.

12. Ms. Asato reads the weather data on her computer.

13. She records a warning on a telephone answering machine.

14. Hundreds of fruit and nut growers call the line.

15. Frost damages young plants and buds on trees.

16. The growers work late into the night.

17. They roll their huge wind machines into the orchards.

18. These giant fans move the air.

19. The movement of the air raises the temperature a few degrees.

20. Wet ground also keeps the temperature higher.

ADDITIONAL PRACTICE
Adverbs

A. Write the adverb in each sentence.

Example:

Settlers waited impatiently at the borders of central Oklahoma.

impatiently

1. At noon on April 22, 1889, the starting guns sounded loudly.

2. The land rush had officially begun.

3. Some settlers rode swiftly.

4. A few of the poorest people ran desperately across the plains.

5. The first settler on each piece of land owned it legally.

6. The swiftest riders quickly reached the lands of their choice.

7. Buggies stopped and hopeful families climbed down.

8. Many lands were already occupied.

9. These settlers had sneaked across.

10. The courts later denied the claims of some of the "Sooners."

B. Write the word in parentheses that best completes each sentence.

Example:

Our cows chew (happy, happily).
happily

11. If corn is (proper/properly) prepared, it makes good winter food for animals.

12. Farm families wait (patiently/patient) for corn to ripen.

13. They work (swift/swiftly) to cut down the stalks.

14. They (careful/carefully) bundle the corn.

15. The wagon full of corn squeaks (noisily/noisy) along.

16. They line a pit (complete/completely) with stones.

17. They work (steady/steadily) to fill it.

18. Then they tramp on the chopped corn (vigorously/vigorous) for a long time.

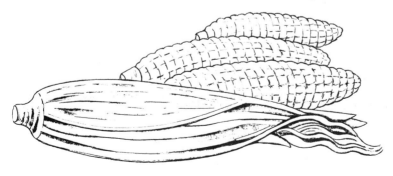

ADDITIONAL PRACTICE
Adverbs That Compare

A. Read each sentence, and write the adverb that compares. Remember to include the word *more* or *most* when it is used.

Example:

Hard coal burns more brightly than soft coal.
more brightly

1. The Bielski family huddled closer.
2. The temperature had dropped faster than anyone could remember.
3. Stan looked the hardest to find wood.
4. Mr. Bielski had driven the farthest of anyone to try to find a job.
5. It was growing colder inside the cabin.
6. Someone knocked louder than a jackhammer on the family's front door.
7. It had frozen harder than ice.
8. They smiled to see Aunt Gail, with Stan grinning the most happily.
9. Mike made the fire burn more briskly.
10. Then Aunt Gail unpacked ham, and Stan ate the most hungrily of all.

B. Write the word or words in parentheses that best completes each sentence.

Example:

The coal-mining song sung (more frequently/most frequently) of all is "John Henry."

most frequently

11. A real miner named John Henry swung his hammer (powerfuller/more powerfully) than any other miner.

12. He drove the steel bar (deeper/deepest) into the coal than his partner did.

13. Some say he worked the (hard/hardest) of all the coal miners in West Virginia.

14. The owners wanted to make money (more quickly/most quickly) than anyone else.

15. A steam drill would drill holes (rapid/more rapidly) than a miner.

16. John Henry said, "I can drive steel (faster/fastest) than that steam drill!"

17. The next day he pounded the steel (farther/farthest) than the steam drill!

ADDITIONAL PRACTICE
Negatives

A. Read each sentence, and write the negative. If the negative is a contraction, write the two words that make up the contraction.

Example:

The Plateau people didn't copy the art of the Northwest Coast people.
didn't—did not

1. Most never carved totem poles.

2. They didn't stay in one place.

3. There isn't any reason to visit berry patches in the springtime.

4. No berries are ripe then.

5. During winter, hunters can't hunt easily in the snowy mountains.

6. Dried salmon doesn't spoil, so the Plateau people could keep it for a long time.

7. Nobody thought winter was a sensible time to travel.

8. Plateau people went nowhere then.

9. Winds did nothing to their log houses.

10. Their summer homes weren't as sturdy as the log houses.

B. Revise each sentence so it becomes a negative statement. You may change any words you need to change.

Example:

My sister and I had an easy time making a totem pole.
My sister and I didn't have an easy time making a totem pole.

11. We found some large cedar trees.

12. We received permission to cut one down.

13. We had cut down a large tree before.

14. Someone helped us move the tree.

15. We were allowed to use my father's tools.

16. My mother let us use her paints.

17. Our first drawing was very good.

18. The eagle looked like an eagle.

19. The bear seemed fierce.

20. The work went very fast.

21. Our totem pole looked exactly like the picture we had drawn.

22. Our totem pole is very tall.

23. We are very pleased with it.

24. My mother asked us to hang it up.

25. She wants everyone to see it.

ADDITIONAL PRACTICE

Too, To, Two

A. Write the word in parentheses that correctly completes each sentence.

Example:

Laura had a snack before she went (too/to/two) bed.
to

1. First, she ate (too/to/two) bananas.

2. Then she went (too/to/two) the bread box.

3. She found (too/to/two) slices of bread inside.

4. She ate a pickle, (too/to/two).

5. She was on her way (too/to/two) bed when she heard a popping sound.

6. Pa had become hungry, (too/to/two).

7. The (too/to/two) of them ate popcorn.

8. Then Laura went (too/to/two) her room.

9. She was (too/to/two) full to sleep.

10. She read (too/to/two) stories by candlelight before falling asleep.

Writing Application Write a paragraph that compares two characters in a story. Use the words *to*, *too*, and *two*.

B. Proofread these sentences. Rewrite correctly each sentence in which *too, to,* or *two* is used incorrectly.

Example:

To birds circle above the prairie.
Two birds circle above the prairie.

11. A weak deer falls too its knees.

12. It can barely walk two the water hole.

13. In to hours, it gets its strength back.

14. Every region has grazing animals, browsing animals, and hunting animals, to.

15. A vulture has to sharp eyes.

16. When one vulture glides down, too or three others will usually follow.

17. Two familiar species in America are the turkey vulture and the black vulture.

18. One vulture is close too extinction.

19. The California condor was once a familiar sight two Native Americans.

20. They gave the name *thunderbird* to the condor.

ADDITIONAL PRACTICE

Good, Well

A. Write the word in parentheses that correctly completes each sentence.

Example:

"This lagoon is a (good/well) place to watch fish," said Linda.
good

1. "These fins should fit you (good/well)," she told Joe.

2. "I can swim (good/well)," he said.

3. "It's still a (good/well) idea to wear a life jacket," she told him.

4. "If you swallow water, you won't be able to swim (good/well)."

5. Linda found a (good/well) mask.

6. Joe could see (good/well) underwater.

7. He got a (good/well) look at the fish.

8. "That one is a (good/well) clown!" said Joe.

9. He was (good/well) at using his snorkel.

10. Later, he ate a (good/well) meal.

B. Proofread these sentences. Rewrite correctly each sentence in which *good* or *well* is used incorrectly.

Example:

My father taught me to tie flies good.
My father taught me to tie flies well.

11. Lake Slo was a well fishing spot.

12. It is a good spot if you're a fish!

13. None of the six of us had well luck.

14. I thought I'd do good because I'd brought thirty of my best flies.

15. "What good flies!" said Aunt Sandra.

16. "How did you do that so good?"

17. "Dad taught me to use good materials," I replied.

18. It's not a well idea to be in the hot sun all day without a hat.

19. The hot dogs we ate for dinner were good.

20. Laverne said, "You did very good today."

ADDITIONAL PRACTICE

They're, Their, There

A. Write the word *they're, their,* or *there* to complete each sentence correctly.

Example:

On the banks of the Jumna River, workers called *dhobis* are doing ____ daily work.
their

1. ____ washing clothes for the people of Delhi, India.

2. They wash clothes on the rocks ____.

3. The dhobis don't earn much, but ____ proud of their work.

4. Many of ____ parents were dhobis.

5. Now ____ worried about pollution.

6. ____ are many factories along the Jumna River.

7. Some pour ____ waste into the river.

8. No matter how hard the dhobis work, ____ not able to get clothes clean.

9. Stronger laws against pollution would keep the river cleaner ____.

10. Then the dhobis could make ____ customers happy again.

B. Proofread these sentences. Rewrite correctly each sentence in which *they're, their,* or *there* is used incorrectly.

Example:

Why are the fourth graders wearing gloves on there hands?
Why are the fourth graders wearing gloves on their hands?

11. Their helping to recycle trash.

12. Students sort they're lunch trash.

13. Paper goes in the can over their.

14. Many students bring there lunches in lunch boxes.

15. Their saving trees.

16. A few students are carrying buckets of food scraps in their hands.

17. They're taking them to the compost pile.

18. They're teacher has helped them learn how to turn garbage into a kind of fertilizer.

19. They have they're own garden section.

20. Their growing tomatoes and corn.

Writing Application All communities have people that do special work for others. Write a few sentences about people who help your community. Use the words *their, they're,* and *there.*

ADDITIONAL PRACTICE
It's, Its

A. Write the word *it's* or *its* to complete each sentence correctly.

Example:

The carp family makes (it's/its) home on four different continents.

its

1. (It's/Its) the largest fish family.

2. (It's/Its) best-known member is the goldfish.

3. A carp has no teeth in (it's/its) jaws.

4. It grinds up (it's/its) food with special teeth in its throat.

5. (It's/Its) a peaceful fish, though.

6. A carp prefers warm, slow-moving water for (it's/its) home.

7. (It's/Its) main food is weeds.

8. In Japan, (it's/its) common to see large, beautiful carp in ponds.

9. A carp in a pond must be protected from (it's/its) natural enemies.

10. (It's/Its) not unusual for large carp to live fifty years or more!

B. Proofread these sentences. Rewrite correctly each sentence in which *it's* or *its* is used incorrectly.

Example:

The train puts on it's lights.
The train puts on its lights.

11. Its beginning to get dark.

12. It's engine hums as the train speeds up the hill.

13. The train carries fifty travelers in its passenger cars.

14. It's dining car is near the caboose.

15. The passengers get off the train at its next stop.

16. Its hard work to unload the luggage.

17. Another train arrives with it's lights on.

18. Its driver has followed the last train.

19. It's clear this is a wilderness train.

20. It's passengers are on a trip through the Rockies.

ADDITIONAL PRACTICE

You're, Your

A. Write the word *you're* or *your* to complete each sentence correctly.

Example:

"You said (you're/your) uncle is a farmer," Masanori said to Van.

your

1. "(You're/Your) right," said Van.

2. "(You're/Your) kidding!" he said.

3. "(You're/Your) uncle's land is underwater!" Masanori continued.

4. "Did you bring (you're/your) fishing pole?" asked Van.

5. "Yes, it's in the back of (you're/your) uncle's car," said Masanori.

6. "(You're/Your) catching dinner," said Van.

7. "(You're/Your) giving me a hint," replied Masanori.

8. Then he exclaimed, "(You're/Your) uncle must be a catfish farmer!"

9. "I know that (you're/your) fond of fish," Van said.

10. "(You're/Your) a true friend for inviting me here," said Masanori.

B. Proofread these sentences. Rewrite correctly each sentence in which *you're* or *your* is used incorrectly.

Example:

You're Thanksgiving dinner is almost ready.
Your Thanksgiving dinner is almost ready.

11. I hear you're aunt made the gravy.

12. I hope you're appetite is good.

13. Your having the biggest turkey I've ever seen!

14. Your Thanksgiving dinners are always a treat.

15. Where are you're plates for setting the table?

16. I'm glad your inviting the neighbors for dinner, too.

17. Your going to enjoy the salad I'm making.

18. Is it true that your serving fish, too?

19. I think you're going to have the best Thanksgiving ever.

Writing Application Give directions that tell someone how to get from one place to another. Use the words *your* and *you're.*

ADDITIONAL PRACTICE
Series Comma

A. Write each sentence. Add commas where they are needed.

Example:

Zimbabwe has grasslands plateaus and a beautiful waterfall.

Zimbabwe has grasslands, plateaus, and a beautiful waterfall.

1. Harare Bulawayo and Nyala are three of its cities.

2. Zimbabwe's four neighbors are Mozambique Zambia Botswana and South Africa.

3. The Ndebele the Shana the Shanga and the Botanga are the main peoples.

4. Zimbabwe has many national parks botanical gardens and recreation areas.

5. Mammals birds and fish are protected.

6. Elephants lions and buffalos are common.

7. Cheetahs hippos and rhinos live there.

8. The most common antelopes are the impala the waterbuck and the greater kudu.

9. Three rare antelopes are the eland the nyala and the klipspringer.

10. In Hwange National Park you may see a giraffe a hyena and a wildebeest.

B. Proofread these sentences. Rewrite them, putting commas in the correct places.

Example:

The green mamba snake is beautiful swift and deadly.

The green mamba snake is beautiful, swift, and deadly.

11. Mambas eat lizards rodents and birds.

12. The green mamba has lime-green skin a long head and a large mouth.

13. Pythons eat rodents lizards and small mammals.

14. They live in Africa Asia and Australia.

15. They attack grab and squeeze their prey.

16. The ball python is a short strong and handsome snake.

17. It eats rats mice and other rodents.

18. The African rock python has black yellow and brown markings.

19. These snakes live in southern Africa eastern Africa northern Africa and Arabia.

20. Poisonous snakes include cobras vipers and rattlesnakes.

21. These snakes are colorful helpful and dangerous.

ADDITIONAL PRACTICE

Commas After Introductory Words and in Direct Address

A. Write the sentences. Insert commas in the correct places.

Example:

"Well you are just a servant!"
"Well, you are just a servant!"

1. "Yes we are going to the ball," said the stepsister to Cinderella.

2. "No you may not go along," she said.

3. "Yes I will scrub the floors."

4. "Well you couldn't go in that, anyway!"

5. "Well our elegant carriage is ready!"

B. Write the sentences, using commas to set off words in direct address.

6. "Mom Cinderella didn't mend my dress!"

7. "There's someone outside Cinderella!"

8. "Welcome our visitor girls!"

9. "Sir I'm sure my foot will fit that slipper."

10. "Young lady I'd like you to try, too," the prince said to Cinderella.

C. Proofread these sentences. Rewrite them so the commas are in the correct places.

Example:

"Yes, our sister, wed the prince."
"Yes, our sister wed the prince."

11. "No we're, not jealous!" said one stepsister.

12. "Sir we, wish her a happy life."

13. "Sister please show this gentleman, to the door!" she continued.

14. "Mom it isn't, fair!" they wailed.

15. "Well let's, just have supper and forget about it."

16. "Yes that's a good, idea!" they said.

17. "Darlings where did you, put my recipe book?" the mother asked.

18. "Here, it is Mother!" they said.

19. "Turn, to the apple recipes dear."

20. "Well someone used up the apples!"

21. "Yes I fed them to, the dog this morning!" giggled the younger girl.

22. "Well perhaps Cinderella will let us, visit her in the palace."

ADDITIONAL PRACTICE
Dialogue and Direct Quotations

A. Write the words spoken directly by a character.

Example:

"Did you see the game?" Susan asked.
"Did you see the game?"

1. "I watched the Tigers," said Alan.

2. "I don't mean major league baseball," Susan said.

3. "I mean the Little League World Series," she said.

4. "Who was playing?" Alan asked.

5. "Panama and Long Beach played," Susan said.

B. Rewrite the sentences. Add quotation marks.

Example:

It was exciting, she said.
"It was exciting," she said.

6. Alan asked, Who were you for?

7. Susan said, I was for Panama.

8. Did they win? asked Alan.

9. Long Beach won, Susan replied.

10. They won twice in a row! she exclaimed.

C. Proofread these sentences. Rewrite them so that each direct quotation is inside quotation marks.

Example:

"Who's the best ball player? asked Jan.
"Who's the best ball player?" asked Jan.

11. "Henry Aaron hit the most home runs in major league history, said Walt."

12. How many did he hit?" she asked.

13. "Walt said, I think he hit 755."

14. You're right, Walt, she said.

15. "I thought it was Babe Ruth, said Elena.

16. Ruth was second," Mrs. Tillman replied."

17. "Have you heard of Josh Gibson? she asked.

18. "He was in the Negro League, said Steve."

19. He may have hit 900 home runs," he added."

20. "What about Sadaharu Oh? asked Jan.

21. "He was Japan's greatest power hitter, she said.

22. "How many home runs did he hit? asked Steve.

23. I know it's over 800, Jan replied."

ADDITIONAL PRACTICE
Titles

A. Write each title correctly.

Example:

Waymon is reading the book Feathers Like a Rainbow
to his younger brother.
Feathers Like a Rainbow

1. Waymon learned about South America by reading the magazine Skipping Stones.

2. When he was younger, he loved the book is your mama a llama?

3. He is learning to play a song from Brazil called Wave.

4. His favorite folktale is a South American story called Josecito the Goat.

5. Waymon just got the magazine Animals.

6. The title of one story is Spectacled Bears of South America.

7. He read about crocodiles in the book reptiles of the world.

8. He likes the poem Crocodile's Toothache.

9. The song Boa Constrictor also makes him laugh.

10. When he saw the movie The Land Before Time, he thought of the rain forest.

B. Rewrite these sentences so that the titles are written correctly.

Example:

Ike has read the book justin morgan had a horse three times.

Ike has read the book <u>Justin Morgan Had a Horse</u> three times.

11. His favorite song is "stewball."

12. He also sings Strawberry Roan.

13. When he was little, his favorite poem was "ride away, ride away."

14. His favorite movie is The Black Stallion.

15. He knows the poem <u>Paul Revere's Ride</u>.

16. Ike got the book "smoky the cowhorse."

17. He will read it as soon as he finishes <u>berchick, my Mother's horse</u>.

18. He plans to read the book Sky Dogs.

19. National Velvet is a movie about children who train a horse.

20. Ike also likes the movie "the man from Snowy River."

21. The magazine National Geographic had an article on wild horses.

22. Sometimes Ike finds articles about horses in the magazine Ranger rick.

Abbreviations

A. For each group of words, choose the abbreviation that is written correctly.

Example:

(Febr./Feb.) 1
Feb.

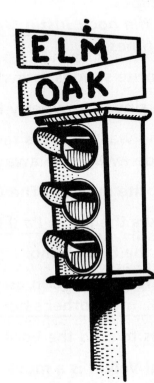

1. (Dr./Doc.) Han

2. Elm (St./Str.)

3. (Unit. St./U.S.) mail

4. (Mstr./Mr.) Kaiser

5. (Ms./Mss.) Lisa Andrews

6. Second (Av./Ave.)

7. (Snt./St.) Patrick's Day

8. (Aug./Agt.) 29

9. 25 Oak (Ro./Rd.)

10. (Tue./Tues.), July 3

Writing Application Write a short letter to a business, asking for information about a product. Use abbreviations where needed.

B. Write each underlined word or group of words as an abbreviation.

Example:

Take North Meridian <u>Road</u> to Will Rogers World Airport.

Rd.

11. My family is visiting Oklahoma in <u>December</u>.

12. Last <u>Sunday</u> I read a book about Will Rogers.

13. My teacher, <u>Doctor</u> Moore, loaned it to me.

14. I picked it up at her house on <u>East</u> Summerlin <u>Avenue</u>.

15. William Penn Rogers was born in Indian Territory, which is now <u>Oklahoma</u>.

16. <u>Mister</u> and Mrs. Rogers had Cherokee ancestors.

17. After working as a cowhand in the <u>United States</u>, Will went to Argentina and worked as a gaucho.

18. Rogers later made comedy films that many Americans watched every <u>Saturday</u> night.